WORLD CATALOGUE OF THESES AND DISSERTATIONS ABOUT THE AUSTRALIAN ABORIGINES AND TORRES STRAIT ISLANDERS

World Catalogue of Theses and Dissertations about the Australian Aborigines and Torres Strait Islanders

W. G. COPPELL

SYDNEY UNIVERSITY PRESS

SYDNEY UNIVERSITY PRESS
Press Building, University of Sydney

UNITED KINGDOM, EUROPE, MIDDLE EAST, AFRICA, CARIBBEAN
Prentice/Hall International, International Book Distributors Ltd
Hemel Hempstead, England
NORTH AND SOUTH AMERICA
International Scholarly Book Services, Inc., Forest Grove, Oregon

National Library of Australia Cataloguing-in-Publication data

Coppell, William George.
    World catalogue of theses and dissertations
    about the Australian Aborigines and Torres
    Strait Islanders.

    Index.
    ISBN 0 424 00039 3.

    [1.] Aborigines, Australian — Bibliography.
    2. Torres Strait Islanders — Bibliography.
    I. Title.

016.301451991094

First published 1977
© W. G. Coppell 1977
This book is funded by money from
THE ELEANOR SOPHIA WOOD BEQUEST
Printed in Australia by Southwood Press Pty Limited, Marrickville, N.S.W.

CONTENTS

ACKNOWLEDGEMENTS

The author of this catalogue is co-author with Ian S. Mitchell of *Education and Aboriginal Australians, 1945-1975: a bibliography* (Centre for the Advancement of Teaching, Macquarie University, in press) and became aware of a number of theses and dissertations which had been written on the education of the Australian Aborigine. He decided to widen his interest to a survey of all theses and dissertations about the Australian Aborigine and later brought this interest to the notice of the Principal of the Australian Institute of Aboriginal Studies. The Institute was able to make available a grant which permitted the completion of this catalogue. The author sincerely acknowledges the encouragement and assistance he received from Dr P. J. Ucko, Principal of the Australian Institute of Aboriginal Studies, Mrs Shirley Andrew, Editor of the Institute, Miss Moira Manning, formerly the Librarian for the Institute, and the Librarian and staff of the Macquarie University Library. Professor R. M. Berndt of the Department of Anthropology, University of Western Australia, also gave considerable assistance and encouragement towards the compilation of the catalogue.

ABBREVIATIONS

DEGREES

B.A.	Bachelor of Arts
B.Ag.Ec.	Bachelor of Agricultural Economics
B.Arch.	Bachelor of Architecture
B.Com.	Bachelor of Commerce
B.D.	Bachelor of Divinity
B.Ed.	Bachelor of Education
B.Historical Sc.	Bachelor of Historical Sciences
B.Juris.	Bachelor of Jurisprudence
B.Litt.	Bachelor of Litérature
B.Med.Sci.	Bachelor of Medical Science
B.Mus.	Bachelor of Music
B.Sc.	Bachelor of Science
B.Soc.St.	Bachelor of Social Studies
B.Soc.Work	Bachelor of Social Work
D.D.S.	Doctor of Dental Science
D.Sc.	Doctor of Science
Dip.Anthrop.	Diploma in Anthropology
Dip.Clinical Psych.	Diploma in Clinical Psychology
Dip.Ed.Admin.	Diploma in Educational Administration
Dip.Lib.	Diploma in Librarianship
Dip.Psych.	Diploma in Psychology
(Hons.)	Degree awarded at Honours level
LL.B.	Bachelor of Laws
LL.M.	Master of Laws
M.A.	Master of Arts
M.Ag.Ec.	Master ofAgricultural Economics
M.App.Sci	Master of Applied Science
M.D.	Doctor of Medicine
M.D.S.	Master of Dental Science
M.Ed.Studies	Master of Educational Studies
M. Fine Arts	Master of Fine Arts
M.Litt.	Master of Literature
M.Phil.	Master of Philosophy
M.Psych.	Master of Psychology
M.Sc.	Master of Science
M.Soc.Admin.	Master of Social Administration
M.Soc.St.	Master of Social Studies
Ph.D.	Doctor of Philosophy

Phil.Fak.Diss.   Philosophische Fakultaet Dissertation
Phil.Fak.Hab.Schr.   Philosophische Fakultaet Habilitations Schrift

PAGINATION DETAILS

diag., diags.	diagram, diagrams
fig., figs.	figure, figures
illus.	illustrated
pl., pls.	plate, plates
pp.	pages
tbl., tbls.	table, tables
v.	volumes

INTRODUCTION

The catalogue

This catalogue is an attempt to provide a fully documented listing of theses and dissertations concerning the Australian Aborigine. The information contained in the catalogue has been obtained from searches carried out in all the main libraries in Australian universities, by correspondence with university librarians and scholars in universities and libraries throughout the world, and from the perusal of other catalogues of theses and dissertations. A provisional checklist of theses and dissertations was compiled and published[1] and as a result some additional information was obtained which has been incorporated into this catalogue.

Some degree of selectivity was used in deciding whether or not to include theses whose primary subjects do not direct themselves to the Australian Aborigine but which have valuable references to the Aborigine. It may well be that some of these marginal works should be omitted in future editions of the catalogue or that other similar theses should be added.

Range of theses and dissertations included in the catalogue

The catalogue is very largely confined to works presented at universities, except that several diploma theses presented at other tertiary education institutions have been included, where they are of particular interest in the field of Aboriginal studies. In addition several theses presented for the Teacher's Higher Certificate of the Education Department of Western Australia have been placed in the catalogue. Diploma and Bachelors' level theses have been listed as it is considered that, although many of these works should be regarded as juvenilia, they are valuable documents, as they may be the initial research documents in many specific subject areas.

---

[1] W. G. Coppell, 'A provisional world checklist of theses concerning the Australian Aborigine', *Australian Institute of Aboriginal Studies, Newsletter*, New Series No. 2, 1974, 32-52.

Cut-off point

The catalogue embraces theses and dissertations concerning Australian Aborigines which have been accepted at the particular universities or other tertiary education institutions to June 1976.

Authors' names

In all but a very few cases it has been possible to provide the authors' full names, as it is considered that by so doing the reader will be more readily able to identify, and, if necessary, trace the authors concerned.

Dating of entries in the catalogue

As far as possible the entries in the catalogue are listed according to the year in which the particular diploma or degree was awarded.

Publications based on theses and dissertations

Frequently theses and dissertations about the Australian Aborigine have not been published, either in whole or part, but wherever possible the authors were asked to provide information about publications based upon the theses and dissertations. However, quite obviously, it has not been possible to ensure that the information provided is exhaustive and the fact that no publications are listed for a particular thesis or dissertation should not be taken to indicate that, in fact, there have been no publications.

The index

The entries in the catalogue are arranged in strict alphabetical order by the authors' surnames, except in the case where a particular author has more than one entry, in which case the entries are arranged in chronological order according to the date on which the degrees were awarded. The entries are cross-indexed under several headings based upon the information contained in the abstracts of the theses or dissertations, or by reference to their texts.

Catalogue

ADAM, Leonhard
Anthropomorphe Darstellungen auf australischen Ritualgeräten.
[Anthropomorphic presentation on Australian (Aboriginal) ritual
implements.]
  Rheinische Friedrich-Wilhelms-Universität, 1957. Phil. Fak. Diss.
  50pp. illus., pls.
  Publication:
  'Anthropomorphe Darstellungen auf Australischen Ritualgeräten',
  Anthropos, 53 (1-2), 1958, 1-50.

ADAM, William
The jaws and dentition of the Tasmanian Aborigines.
  University of Melbourne, 1940. D.D.S. 165pp. illus., tbls.

ADAMS, E. Jean
Changes in Wikmunkan kinship structure: an introductory analysis.
  Monash University, 1970. B.A. (Hons.). 82pp. figs., map.

AKERMAN, Kim
Death and the significance of disposal methods and mortuary rites in
Aboriginal Australia.
  University of Western Australia, 1969. B.Sc. iii, 60pp. figs.

ALEXANDER, Diane Helen
Yarrabah Aboriginal English.
  University of Queensland, 1969. B.A. (Hons.). xiv, 149pp. maps.

Woorabinda Aboriginal English: a study of the salient linguistic
differences between the Aboriginal and non-Aboriginal English speech
of informants on Woorabinda Aboriginal settlement in Central
Queensland.
  University of Queensland, 1968. M.A. xiv, 188pp. maps.

ALLEN, Frederick James
Archaeology and the history of Port Essington.
  Australian National University, 1969. Ph.D. 2 v. (vi, 445 pp.).
  maps, pls.

Publications:
'Port Essington: a successful limpet port?', *Historical Studies*, 15, 1972,
   342-60.
'The archaeology of nineteenth-century British imperialism: an
   Australian case study, *World Archaeology*, 5 (1), 1973, 44-50.

ALLEN, Harry R.
Western plain and eastern hill: a reconstruction of the subsistence
activities of the Aboriginal inhabitants of central eastern Australia.
   University of Sydney, 1968. B.A. (Hons.). vi, 110pp. illus., maps.

_____

Where the crow flies backwards: man and land in the Darling basin.
   Australian National University, 1972. Ph.D. vi, 382, 44pp. diags.,
   maps, pls. tbls.

ALPHER, Barry Jacob
Son of ergative: the Yir Yoront language of northeast Australia.
   Cornell University, 1973. Ph.D.xii, 412pp. maps.

ANDERSON, John Robert
The quaternary geology and sedimentology of the Gallus sites at Keilor.
   University of Melbourne, 1972. B.Sc.(Hons.). ix, 111pp. diag.,
   figs., maps, pls., tbls.

ANELL, Bengt
Contribution to the history of fishing in the southern seas.
   University of Uppsala, 1955, Ph.D. 247pp. illus., figs., maps, pls.

ARMSTRONG, Gowan
Social change at Maningrida.
   University of Sydney, 1967. Dip. Anthrop. 90,3,4,5,2pp. diags,
   maps, tbls.

ARMSTRONG, Russell Edward McDonald
The dispossession of the Kalkadoons.
   University of New England, 1974. 2 v. (iv, 226pp.). maps, pls.

ASHBOLT, Kerry C.
Identification of artefacts.
   University of Sydney, 1967. B.A. (Hons.). 44pp. illus., tbl.

ASHLEY-MONTAGU, Montague Francis
Coming into being among the Australian Aborigines: a study of the
procreative beliefs of the native tribes of Australia.

Columbia University, 1937. Ph.D. 355pp. figs., maps.
Publication:
Coming into being among the Australian Aborigines: a study of the
procreative beliefs of the native tribes of Australia. London, G.
Routledge and Sons, 1937. xxxv, 362pp.

ASHTON, Shirley E.
The failure of the Buntingdale Mission and the Port Phillip
Protectorate: some aspects of Aboriginal-European contact.
University of Melbourne, 1965. B.A. (Hons.). 55pp.

BAILEY, Geoffrey Nigel
The role of shell middens in prehistoric economies.
Cambridge University, 1975. Ph.D. 2 v. (various pagings). illus.,
maps, pls., tbls.

BAIN, Margaret
At the interface: Aboriginal and white contact in Australia.
Monash University, 1972. M.A. preliminary essay. 2, 123pp.

BAKER, Margaret
A social survey of Tingha.
University of Sydney, 1943. M.A. 92, [9]pp. figs, map, tbls.

BAKHTA, Vladimir M.
The communal system of production of the Australian Aborigines and
the Papuans of eastern New Guinea: a comparative analysis.
Moscow M.V. Lomonosov State University, 1963. B. Historical Sc.
379pp.

BAKKER, Henny
Assimilation and the effects of the Act.
University of Queensland, 1965. B.Soc.St. [2],43pp. diags., illus.,
tbls.

BAMBOROUGH, Thomas Henry
An investigation of school-community relations in Walgett, New South
Wales.
University of New England, 1960. Dip. Ed. Admin. 34,7pp.

BARBER, Ross
Capital punishment in Queensland.
University of Queensland, 1967. B.A. (Hons.). ii, 218pp. illus., tbls.

BARBETTI, Michael Francis
Archeomagnetic and radiocarbon studies of Aboriginal fire-places.
Australian National University, 1974. Ph.D.xiii, 164, 33pp. figs.,
illus., pls., tbls.
Publications:
with M. W. McElhinny, 'Evidence of a geomagnetic excursion 30,000
yr. B.P.', *Nature*, 239, 1972, 327-30.
with M. W. McElhinny, 'The Lake Mungo geomagnetic excursions',
Philosophical Transactions of the Royal Society of London, 281
(1305), 1976, 515-42. figs., tbl.
with M. Allen, 'Prehistoric man at Lake Mungo, Australia, by 32,000 yr
B.P.', *Nature*, 240, 1972, 46-8.

BARKER, Geoffrey; DONALD, Robert; MOORE, David and
RAHILL, Michael
Koories, housing, society and the future.
University of Melbourne, 1975. B.Arch. 288pp. figs., tbls.

BARKER, Graham H.
Totemism and totemic affiliation in Australian Aboriginal society: a
discussion.
Macquarie University, 1974. B.A. (Hons.). iv, 133, [6]pp. tbls.

BARKER, Robert Jamieson
The effectiveness of a language development programme in part-
Aboriginal children.
University of Melbourne, 1970. Dip.Psych. iv, 24pp.

BARTHOLOMEUSZ, Roland K.
The peopling of Aboriginal Australia.
University of Western Australia, 1971. B.Sc. v, 63pp. maps, tbls.

BARWICK, Diane Elizabeth
A little more than kin: regional affiliation and group identity among
Aboriginal migrants in Melbourne.
Australian National University, 1963. Ph.D. xxvi,400,7pp. figs.,
maps, tbls.

BAUER, Francis Harry
The regional geography of Kangaroo Island, South Australia.
Australian National University, 1959. Ph.D. xxiii, 712 pp. illus.,
maps, pls., tbls.

BEALE, Tony
The Mari language.
    Australian National University, 1975. B.A. (Hons.). 92, [65]pp.
    diags., maps, tbls.

BEATTY, Kenneth Herbert
An Aboriginal minority in Australia: an examination of assimilation in
the light of its problems and alternative policies.
    University of Western Australia, 1965. B.Sc. vi, 53, [7]pp.

BEAUCHAMP, Alice Ester
The social relationship of white and coloured children in the sixth class
at La Perouse Public School.
    University of Sydney, 1953. B.A. (Hons.). iv,124,3pp. diag., map,
    tbls.

BECKENHAM, Percy William John
The education of the Australian Aborigine.
    University of Melbourne, 1946. B.Ed. 219pp.
Publication:
The education of Australian Aborigines. Melbourne, Australian
    Council of Educational Research, 1948. 58pp. map.

BECKETT, Jeremy Rex
A study of a mixed-blood Aboriginal minority in the pastoral west of
New South Wales.
    Australian National University, 1958. M.A. 296, [8]pp. diag., map,
    pls., tbls.

Politics in the Torres Straits Islands.
    Australian National University, 1963. Ph.D. 5, [4], 403pp. maps,
    tbls.

BELL, Diane Robin
From moth hunters to blacktrackers: an interpretive analysis of the
black and white experience.
    Monash University, 1975. B.A. (Hons.). 102pp. map, tbls.
Appendix 1: A reconstruction and discussion of the life style of the
Ngunawal of south east Australia.
    43, iv, iii pp. maps, music, notation, tbls.

BELL, James Harle
The La Perouse Aborigines: a study of their group life and assimilation
into modern Australian society.

University of Sydney, 1959. Ph.D. vi, 470pp. diags., maps, pls., tbls.
Publications:
'Official policies toward the Aborigines of New South Wales', *Mankind*, 1959, 345-55.
'Some demographic and cultural characteristics of the La Perouse Aborigines', *Mankind*, 1961, 425-38.

BELL, Kenneth J.
Natives of the Pinjarra area.
  Education Department of Western Australia, Teacher's Higher Certificate thesis, 1966. 68pp.

BELSHAW, James Drummond
The economic basis of Aboriginal life in northern New South Wales in the nineteenth century.
  University of New England, 1966. B.A.(Hons.). [125]pp. maps, pls.

BERN, John Edward
Blackfella business, white fella law: political struggle and competition in a south-east Arnhem Land Aboriginal community.
  Macquarie University, 1974. Ph.D. vi, 490pp. diags., maps.

BICKFORD, R. Anne
The traditional economy of the Aborigines of the Murray Valley.
  University of Sydney, 1966. B.A.(Hons.). x, 198pp. maps, pls.

BICKNELL, Peter Ernest
The contribution of the concept of 'task' to an understanding of the problems facing urban Aboriginal families.
  Flinders University, 1973. M.Soc.Admin. iv, 72pp.

BIDDLE, Ellen Horgan
The assimilation of Aborigines in Brisbane, Australia, 1965.
  University of Missouri, 1969. Ph.D. xi, 263pp. illus., tbls.
Publication:
with Hazel Smith, 'Educational standards for Aboriginals', *The Australian Journal of Social Issues*, 3 (4), 1968, 13-25.

BIRDSALL, Christina
Bilingual and preschool education as they relate to Aboriginal education.
  University of Western Australia, 1976. B.A. 60pp.

BIRDSELL, Joseph Benjamin
The trihybrid origin of the Australian Aborigine.
Harvard University, 1941. Ph.D. 257pp. maps, pls., tbls.
Publication:
'A preliminary report on the trihybrid origin of the Australian
Aborigines', *American Journal of Physical Anthropology*, 28, 1941,
6.

BIRK, David Barry Wilson
The Malak Malak language, Daly River (Western Arnhem Land).
Australian National University, 1976. Ph.D. xii, 242pp. map.

BIRTLES, Terry G.
A survey of land use, settlement and society in the Atherton-Evelyn
district, north Queensland, 1880-1914.
University of Sydney, 1973. M.A. xxiv, 370pp. figs., illus., tbls.

BISKUP, Peter
Native administration and welfare in Western Australia, 1897-1954.
University of Western Australia, 1965. M.A. 498pp. tbls.
Publication:
*Not slaves, not citizens: the Aboriginal problems in Western Australia,
1898-1954.* St. Lucia, University of Queensland Press, 1973. 324pp.
illus., tbls.

BLADEL, Frances M.
British-Tasmanian relations between 1803-1828.
University of Tasmania, 1970. B.A. (Hons.). 11,77pp. illus., map.

BLAESS, Frederick John Henry
The Evangelical Lutheran Synod in Australia Inc. and mission work
amongst the Australian natives in connection with the Dresden
(Leipzig) Lutheran Mission Society, 1838-1900.
Concordia Seminary, St Louis, Missouri, 1941 B D 153pp

BLAKE, Barry John
A brief description of the Kalkatungu language.
Monash University, 1967. M.A. (Hons.) xvi, 119pp. figs., map.
Publication:
The Kalkatungu language: A brief description. Canberra, Australian
Institute of Aboriginal Studies, 1969. (Australian Aboriginal Studies
No. 20, Linguistic Series No. 8) 133pp. graphs, illus., map.

The case systems of Australian Aboriginal languages. Monash
University, 1975. Ph.D.xii, 356pp.

BLOWS, Johanna Mieke
A comparative study of the Gunabibi-Gadjari complex in four Aboriginal tribes of the Northern Territory.
University of Sydney, 1968. B.A. (Hons.). 84, [4]pp. tbls.

BLUNDELL, Valda J.
Aboriginal adaptation in northwest Australia.
University of Wisconsin, 1975. Ph.D. 3 v. (xxxvi, 821pp.). diags., maps, pls., tbls.

BOLTON, Geoffrey Curgenven
A survey of the Kimberley pastoral industry from 1885 to the present.
University of Western Australia, 1953. M.A. (Hons.). 339pp. maps, pls.

BONESS, Neil D.
Desert adze to woodland adze: a study of available ethnographic data to determine the functions of stone tools in selected environmental areas.
University of Sydney, 1971. B.A. 74pp. maps (including one folder), pls., tbls.

BOORSBOOM, Adrianus Petrus
Jabudurawa: post-begrafenis ritueel in Arnhem Land.
[Jabudurawa: post-burial rituals in Arnhem Land.]
Katholieke Universiteit, Nijmegen, 1972. Doctooral Scriptie (approximately equivalent to M.A.). 64pp.

BOSLER, Wendy
The Keilor archaeological sites: an historical survey.
Australian National University, 1975. B.A. (Hons.). 69pp. pls.

BOWDLER, Sandra
Bass Point: the excavation of a south-east Australian shell midden showing cultural and economic change.
University of Sydney, 1970. B.A. (Hons.). 141pp. figs., maps, pls., tbls.

BOYALL, Jan F.
The sanction of the supernatural in primitive societies.
University of Sydney, 1950. B.A. [8],124pp.

BRANDL, Erhard J.
Art in Australian Aboriginal society and culture: an approach to the art of non-literate peoples.
University of Western Australia, 1967. B.A. xiv,74pp. map, pls.

BRANDL, Maria M.
Pukumani, the social content of bereavement in a north Australian tribe.
University of Western Australia, 1971. Ph.D. 564pp. maps, pls., tbls.

BRASCH, Sarah
Gureng: a language of the upper Burnett River, south-east Queensland.
Australian National University, 1975. B.A. (Hons.). 2 v. (various pagings). map.

BRAYSHAW, Helen C.
Some aspects of the material culture of the Aborigines of the Hunter valley at the time of the first white settlement.
University of New England, 1966. B.A. (Hons.). 186pp. maps, pls.

BREEN, John Gavan
A description of the Waluwara language.
University of Melbourne, 1971. M.A. 306pp.

BREEN, Robin Madeleine
The rainbow-serpent as a symbol in Aboriginal religion.
University of Queensland, 1969. B.A. (Hons.). 74,[5], 193pp. maps.

An assessment of the adult education needs of urbanizing Aborigines in Charleville, south west Queensland.
University of Queensland, 1976. M.A. iii, 193pp.

BREMER, Hanna
Zur Morphologie von Zentralaustralien.
[The morphology of Aborigines of Central Australia]
Karl-Ruprecht-Universität, Heidelberg, 1966. Phil.Fak.Hab.Schr. 270pp.

BRICE, Grizel Anne
The interpretation of the art of the hunting societies of Europe and Australia.
University of New England, 1965. B.Litt. 141, [3]pp.

BRIDGES, Barry John
Aboriginal and white relations in New South Wales, 1788-1855.
University of Sydney, 1966. M.A. 3 v. (xxiv, 1210pp.), tbls.

BRISBOUT, Michelle
The peopling of Australia — a resume of the technological, skeletal and genetic/linguistic material from Australia and south east Asia.
University of Western Australia, 1976. B.A. 43pp.

BROCK, Margaret S.
Bantu and Aborigines: a comparative study of government policies in South Africa and Australia (with particular reference to South Australia).
University of Adelaide, 1969. B.A. (Hons.). 133pp. map.

BRODIE, Jillian Jean
Integration for South Australian Aborigines.
Flinders University, 1971. B.A. xi, 75pp.

BROWN, Helen
Settlement in the Maranoa district, 1842-1879.
University of Queensland, 1963. B.A. (Hons.). 80pp. maps.

BROWN, Maxwell Walter
Totemism in Australia
University of Western Australia, 1964. B.A. iii, 48pp.

BROWN, Tasman
Cranio-facial variations in a central Australian tribe: a radiographic investigation of young adult males and females.
University of Adelaide, 1965. M.D.Sc. xii, 182pp. diags., illus., tbls.
Publication:
Cranio-facial variations in a central Australian tribe: a radiographic investigation of young adult males and females. Adelaide, Library Board of South Australia, 1965. 182pp. bibliog., figs., glossary, tbls.

Skull of the Australian Aboriginal: a multivariate analysis of craniofacial associations.
University of Adelaide, 1967. D.D.S. xiii, 236pp. diags., graphs, pls, tbls.
Publication:
Morphology of the Australian skull: studied by multivariate analysis. Canberra, Australian Institute of Aboriginal Studies, 1973. (Australian Aboriginal Studies No. 49.) 140pp.

BROWN, Tom Austen
Type and group in prehistory.
University of Sydney, 1974. B.A. (Hons.). 152pp.

BRUELL, Peter
Dareton and Aborigines: a feasibility study for a community health centre.
> University of Melbourne, 1975. B.Arch. 88pp. illus., maps, plans, pls., tbls.

BULL, Margaret
Kurrawang Mission and the future of its children: a study of the adjustment of Australian Aboriginal children to the wider Australian community.
> Education Department of Western Australia, Teacher's Higher Certificate thesis, 1961. 107pp. pls.

BURNARD, Sally
Government policy and Aboriginal mission stations, South Australia.
> University of Adelaide, 1961. B.A. (Hons.). 216pp. pls, maps.

BURRAGE, Winifred Mary
The education of the half-caste Aborigine: a study of the education past, present and future, of the half-caste Aborigines of Australia with special reference to those in New South Wales.
> University of Melbourne, 1938. B.Ed. 82pp. diags., pls.

BURY, Warren Richard
The foundation of the Point McLeay Aboriginal Mission.
> University of Adelaide, 1964. B.A. (Hons.). 128pp. maps, pls.

BUSBY, Frank; HAMPTON, Tony and POWER, Shane
Aboriginal housing Dareton: a case study.
> University of Melbourne, 1975. B.Arch. 5 v. (486pp). figs., illus., maps, plans, pls, tbls.

BUSCOMBE, Eve
Artists and their sitters: a colonial portrait. A guide to the portrait painters of New South Wales and Van Diemen's Land, 1820-1850.
> Australian National University, 1970. M.A. 5v. (iv, 343pp.). illus., portraits.

BUXTON, Gordon Leslie
Land and people: a study of settlement and society in the Riverina, 1861-1891.
> Australian National University, 1965. Ph.D. xii, 473pp. illus., pls., tbls.

CAKE, Graeme Henry
An examination of the identification, adjustment, adaptation and acceptance of the residents of the Katukutu Aboriginal Young Men's Hostel in Mt. Lawley, Western Australia.
University of Western Australia, 1963, B.A. v, 104pp. fig., pls.

CALLEY, Malcolm John Chalmers
Religion and art: their nature and inter-relationship.
University of Sydney, 1952. B.A. xviii, 102, [5]pp. pls.

Aboriginal pentacostalism: a study of changes in religion, North Coast, New South Wales.
University of Sydney, 1955. M.A. xxii, 146pp. illus., map.

Bandjalang social organization.
University of Sydney, 1959. Ph.D. 254, xxxi pp. maps, tbls.

CAMPBELL, Ian C.
The relations between settlers and Aborigines in the pastoral district of New England, 1832-1860.
University of New England, 1969. B.A. (Hons.). iv. 82pp. maps, pls.

CAMPBELL, Raymond
The Aborigine and his education in New South Wales.
University of Melbourne, 1947. B.Ed. 157pp. maps, pls., tbls.
Includes appendix of art work in various media by Aboriginal and part-Aboriginal children.

CAMPBELL, Thomas Draper
Dentition and palate of the Australian Aborigine.
University of Adelaide, 1925. D.D.S. 2 v. (viii, 123pp.). figs., maps, pls., tbls.
Publication:
Dentition and palate of the Australian Aboriginal. Adelaide, The Hassell Press. 1925, (University of Adelaide Publications under the Keith Sheridan Foundation No. 1) viii, 123pp. figs., maps, pls., tbls.

Collection of (37) published papers on original field research (mainly on certain aspects of the biology of living Australian Aborigines).
University of Adelaide, 1939. D.Sc. 2 v. (146pp.). pls.

CAMPBELL, Valerie M.
A field survey of shell middens of the lower McLeay Valley, with special reference to their potential and possible methods of investigation.
  University of New England, 1969. B.A.(Hons.). [6], vi, 106, [2]pp. maps, pls., tbls.

CARLYON, Norman Murdoch
G.A. Robinson — Chief Protector.
  University of Melbourne, 1960. B.A.(Hons.). 115,4,3, [8]pp. figs., pls.

CARR, John Arnold
The history and work of the Narrogin and Districts Native Council.
  Education Department of Western Australia, Teacher's Higher Certificate thesis, 1966. 63pp.

CAWTE, John E.
Australian ethnopsychiatry and frontier psychiatry. Vol. 1: Psychiatric aspects of the human ecology of the Australian outback. Vol. 2: The serpent and the tide: culture contact and mental health in Australian Aborigines.
  University of New South Wales, 1969. Ph.D. 2 v. (various pagings), figs., tbls.
Publications:
Cruel, poor and brutal nations. Honolulu, University of Hawaii Press, 1972. xv, 183pp.
Medicine is the law: studies in the psychiatric anthropology of Australian tribal society. Honolulu, University of Hawaii Press, 1973. xxiv, 260pp. illus.

CHADWICK, Neil
A descriptive study of the Djingili language, Northern Territory.
  University of New England, 1968. M.A. 321pp.
Publication:
A descriptive study of the Djingili language. Canberra, Australian Institute of Aboriginal Studies, 1975. xiii, 130pp. charts, map.

CHAMBERS, Barbara
Attitude changes in teachers' college students towards Aborigines: the effect of an Aboriginal studies course on the attitudes of third year teachers' college students towards Aborigines.
  University of New England, 1971. B.Ed. vii, 152pp. tbls.

CHASE, Athol
The Australian Aborigine: his place in evolutionary anthropology.
  University of Queensland, 1970. B.A. (Hons). iv, 122pp.

CHENG, Peter Chung Kwong
Dental-arch morphology of Australian Aborigines: a metric study of arch size and shape.
  University of Adelaide, 1972. M.D.S. 179pp. figs., illus., tbls.

CHIA, Ah Tee
Architecture and the Aborigines: architecture as a catalyst in social motivation.
  University of Queensland, 1971. B.Arch. iv, 222pp. diags., maps, tbls.

CHRISTOPHERS, Robin
A survey of Aborigines in Claremont Mental Hospital, 1965.
  University of Western Australia, 1965, Dip. Clinical Psych. 75pp. tbls.

CLARKE, Gladys
The early treatment of the Aborigines, 1788-1842.
  University of New England, 1956. B.A. 85, 111pp.

CLARK, Helen M.
Aboriginal assimilation in two communities.
  University of Newcastle, 1971, M.Sc. vii, 192pp. diags., tbls.

CLEVERLY, John Robert
A preliminary study of the phonology and grammar of Djamindjung.
  University of New England, 1969. M.A. [4], 218pp. map.

COLEMAN, Emily
An analysis of small samples from the West Point shell midden.
  University of Sydney, 1966. B.A. (Hons.). 84, [26]pp. illus., pls., tbls.

COLLIER, Mary
Cemetery Point: the analysis and economic interpretation of a midden.
  Australian National University, 1975. B.A. (Hons.). 43pp. pls.

COLLING, Penelope
The Myall Creek massacre — an episode in the relations between the settlers and the Australian Aborigines, 1838.
  University of Melbourne, 1962. B.A. (Hons.). 61pp.

COOK, Pamela Wake
A survey of the Mogumber Methodist Training Centre.
University of Western Australia, 1967. B.A. iv, 55pp. pls.

COOLICAN, Raphael Edward
Morbidity in an Australian rural practice.
University of New South Wales, 1971. M.D. 2 v. ([5], vi, 251, [9];
[85]pp.). map, pls., tbls.

COOPER, Carol Patricia
The Beechworth collection of Aboriginal artefacts.
Australian National University, 1975. B.A.(Hons.). vi, 106,
[16]pp. illus., maps, pls., tbls.

CORRIS, Peter R.
Aborigines and Europeans in western Victoria from first contacts to
1860.
Monash University, 1966. M.A.(Hons.). v, 245pp. maps, tbls.
Publication:
Aborigines and Europeans in western Victoria. Canberra, Australian
Institute for Aboriginal Studies, 1968. 178pp. maps.

COTTERELL, John L.
Some effects of the introduction of literature in the homes of
Aboriginal children aged six to ten years.
University of Queensland, 1975. M.Ed.Studies. 83pp.

COUTTS, Peter John Fraser
The archaeology of Wilson's Promontory.
Australian National University, 1967. M.A. various pagings, illus.,
maps, tbls.
Publications:
The archaeology of Wilson's Promontory. Canberra, Australian
Institute of Aboriginal Studies, 1970 (Australian Aboriginal Studies
No. 28) xvi, 153pp. pls., figs., tbls., bibliog.

COWELL, Geoffrey
The attitude of Alexander Harris and others and general Australian
attitudes to the Aborigines and other races between 1820 and 1840 as
revealed in their works.
University of New England, 1972. B.A.(Hons.). iv, 96pp.

COWIN, Winifred
European-Aboriginal relations in early Queensland, 1859-1897.
University of Queensland, 1950. B.A. iv, 122pp.

CRAN, James Alexander
An investigation of the effect of dietary changes on the oral tissues of central Australian Aborigines.
University of Adelaide, 1960. Part 2 of D.D.S. various pagings. map, pls., collection of papers.

CRAVEN, Arthur Harry
A cephalometric investigation of central Australian Aborigines using a Roentgenegraphic technique.
University of Illinois, 1952. M.A. 56pp. diags., tbls.

CRAWFORD, Ian M.
The Kurnai tribe in Gippsland: an interpretation of tribal life.
University of Melbourne, 1958. B.A. (Hons.). 29, [5]pp. illus., maps, pls.

Late prehistoric changes in Aboriginal culture in Kimberley, Western Australia.
University of London, 1969. Ph.D. 364pp. diags., illus., map, pls.

CRIM, Donald Emerson
Changes in kin-term usages in the Aboriginal community at Mitchell River Mission, northern Queensland.
Cornell University, 1973. Ph.D. 108pp.

CRISP, Brian R.
Totemism in Aboriginal Australia.
University of Western Australia, 1963. B.A. (Hons.). 37pp.

CROSS, Kenneth Stuart
Biometrical study of the relative degree of purity of race of the Tasmanian, Australian and Papuan.
University of Melbourne, 1910. M.D. Collection of published papers submitted for degree of M.D.

CUMMINGS, Barbara Joy
The failure of Aboriginal children in New South Wales schools: is pre-school education the solution?
University of Sydney, 1974. B.A. (Hons.). 219pp. figs., tbls.

CUNNINGHAM, Margaret Clare
Alawa phonology and grammar
University of Queensland, 1969. Ph.D. xiv, 300pp. map.

Publication:
Alawa phonology and grammar. Canberra, Australian Institute of
Aboriginal Studies, 1972. (Australian Aboriginal Studies No. 37)
189pp. illus., figs., tbls., bibliog.

CURTHOYS, Ann
Race and ethnicity: a study of the response of British colonists to
Aborigines, Chinese and non-British Europeans in New South Wales,
1856-1881.
Macquarie University, 1973. Ph.D. 713pp.

DALLAS, Mary
The criss-cross quiz: an approach to Aboriginal bark painting.
University of Sydney, 1973, B.A. (Hons.). 103pp. figs. music, pls.,
tbls.

DALTON, Peter Richard
A survey of the effects of unemployment on a settlement of part-
Aboriginals at Allawah Grove, Western Australia.
University of Western Australia, 1959. B.A. 22pp. tbl.

_____

Broome, a multiracial community: a study of social and cultural
relationships in a town in the West Kimberleys, Western Australia.
University of Western Australia, 1964. M.A. x, 257pp. illus., map,
pls.

DASEN, Pierre R.
Cognitive development in Aborigines of Central Australia: concrete
operations and perceptual activities.
Australian National University, 1970. Ph.D. xiii, 385pp. diags.,
figs., tbls.
Publications:
'Cross-cultural Piagetian research: a summary', *Cross-cultural
Psychology,* 3 (1), 1972. 23 39.
Reprinted in J. W. Berry and P. R. Dasen, *Human development. A
Random House annual, 1972.* New York, Random House, 1975,
pp.409-23.
'The development of conservation in Aboriginal children: a rep-
lication study', *International Journal of Psychology,* 1972, 75-85.
'The influence of ecology, culture and European contact on cognitive
development in Australian Aborigines' in J. W. Berry and P. R.
Dasen (eds.), *Culture and cognition: readings in cross-cultural
psychology.* London, Methuen, 1973, pp.381-408.

'Piagetian research in Central Australia' in G. E. Kearney, P. R. de Lacey and G. R. Davidson (eds.), *The psychology of Aboriginal Australians*. Sydney, Wiley, 1973, pp.89-96.

with P. R. de Lacey and G. N. Seagrim, 'An investigation of reasoning ability in adopted and fostered Aboriginal children' in G. E. Kearney, P. R. de Lacey and G. R. Davidson (eds.), *The psychology of Aboriginal Australians*. Sydney, Wiley, 1973, pp.97-104.

Biologie ou culture? La psychologie inter-ethnique d'un point de vue Piagétian, *Psychologie Canadienne*, 14 (2), 1973, 149-66.

DAVIDSON, Daniel Sutherland
Critique of theories of social organization in Australia.
 University of Pennsylvania, 1924. M.A. 75pp.
Publication:
'The basis of social organization in Australia', *American Anthropologist*, 27, 1926, 529-48.

The chronological aspects of certain Australian social institutions inferred from geographical distribution.
 University of Pennsylvania, 1928. Ph.D. 147pp. illus., maps, pls.
Publication:
The chronological aspects of certain Australian social institutions as inferred from geographical distribution. Philadelphia, 1928. 147pp.

DAVIDSON, Graham Robert
Myers reinterpreted: a study of choice reaction times in an Aboriginal and white Australian group.
 University of Queensland, 1971. B.A.(Hons.). vi, 47pp. figs., tbls.

Culture learning through caretaker-child interchange behavior.
 University of Queensland, 1976. Ph.D. 17, 295pp. figs., pls., tbls.

DAVIDSON, John Arthur
Attitudes of Aboriginal children to education.
 University of Queensland, 1966. B.A. x, 47, [19]pp. diags, tbls.

DAVIES, Bronwyn
The part-Aboriginal child in the Australian classroom.
 University of New England, 1974. B.Ed. 124pp. diag., illus., tbls.
  The reference librarian of the University of New England reported 'that neither Ms Davies nor her supervisor can lay their hands on a copy of her thesis'.

DAVIVONGS, Virapunt
The pelvic girdle and femur of the Australian Aborigine.
University of Adelaide, 1962. M.Sc. 119pp. diags., illus., pls., tbls.

DEAKIN, Hilton
Elders learn a new game: a study of manipulation at two missions in the
Kimberley Division, Western Australia.
Monash University, 1973. B.A. (Hons.). 88pp.

DEERING, Irene Yvonne
A study of the Australian Aboriginal myth of the rainbow-serpent.
Monash University, 1974. B.A. (Hons.). 112pp. tbls.

DE GRAAF, Mark
Totemism in the Western Desert of Australia.
University of Western Australia, 1970. B.A. 36pp.

DE LACEY, Philip R.
Milieu, race and classificatory ability in Australia.
University of New England, 1969. Ph.D. 248pp. diags., map, pls.,
tbls.
Publications:
'A cross-cultural study of classifactory ability in Australia', *Journal of
Cross-Cultural Psychology*, 1970 (1), 293-304. Reprinted in
(a) J. W. Berry and P. R. Dasen (eds.), *Culture and cognition.*
London, Methuen, 1973. pp.353-63.
(b) G. E. Kearney, P. R. de Lacey and G. R. Davidson (eds.), *The
psychology of Aboriginal Australians.* Sydney, Wiley, 1973. pp.59-
70.
'An index of contact for Aboriginal communities', *Australian Journal of
Social Issues*, 1970 (5), 219-23.

DE LAWYER, Antonia
Davenport and Umeewarra since 1937.
University of Adelaide, 1972. B.A. (Hons.). v, 120pp.

DE LEMOS, Marion Molly Murray Pereira
The development of the concept of conservation in Australian
Aboriginal children.
Australian National University, 1966. Ph.D. xiii, 464pp. figs., pls.,
tbls.
Publications:
'The development of conservation in Aboriginal children', *Interna-
tional Journal of Psychology*, 4 (4), 1969, 255-9. (Also reprinted in

G. E. Kearney, P. R. de Lacey and G. R. Davidson (eds.), *The psychology of Aboriginal Australians*. Sydney, Wiley, 1973.
'Conceptual development in Aboriginal children. Implications for Aboriginal education' in S. S. Dunn and C. M. Tatz, *Aborigines and education*. Melbourne, Sun Books, 1969. xi, 366pp.

DENHAM, Woodrow Wilson
The detection of patterns in Alyawara nonverbal behaviour.
University of Washington, 1973. Ph.D. ix, 229pp. graphs, maps, pls.

DENHOLM, David
Some aspects of squatting in New South Wales and Queensland, 1847-1864.
Australian National University, 1972. Ph.D. xx, 384pp. figs., graphs, illus., maps, tbls.

D'ESPEISSIS, Jan L.
The occurrence of the Gurangara petroglyphs in Western Australia.
University of Western Australia, 1972. B.A. 52pp. figs., maps.

DE ZWAAN, Jan Daniel
A preliminary analysis of Gogo-Yimidjir: a study of the structure of the primary dialect of the Aboriginal language spoken at the Hopevale Mission in North Queensland.
University of Queensland, 1967. M.A qualifying essay. xv, 239pp. tbls.
Publication:
A preliminary analysis of Gogo-Yimidjir: a study of the primary dialect of the Aboriginal language spoken in Hopevale Mission in North Queensland. Canberra, Australian Institute of Aboriginal Studies, 1969. (Australian Aboriginal Studies No. 16, Linguistic Series No. 5) 168pp. tbls., bibliog.

An analysis of the Gogo-Yimidjir language: a depth study of the structure of the primary dialect of the Aboriginal language spoken at the Hopevale Mission in North Queensland.
University of Queensland, 1969. Ph.D. 3v (xxiii, 436; viii, 456pp.); pls., tbls., tape.

DIGNAN, Donald Keith
Economic and social development in the Lower Burnett, 1840-1960: a regional study with special reference to the Kolan Shire and the Gin Gin District.
University of Queensland, 1962. M.A. ix, 197, [7]pp. tbls.

DIX, Warwick C.
Technical education in technological change, with particular reference to the Australian Aboriginal and mixed blood population in Western Australia.
University of Western Australia, 1960. B.A. 36pp.

DIXON, Robert Malcolm Ward
The Dyirbal language of north Queensland.
University of London, 1967. Ph.D. 484pp. map.
Publication:
The Dyirbal language of north Queensland. Cambridge University Press, 1972. xxiv, 420pp. illus., map.

DONALD, Robert *see* BARKER, Geoffrey, *et al.*

DROBEC, Eric
Medizinmannwesen, Krankheitszauber und Heilkunde bei den australischen Eingeborenen.
[Magic of illness and medical science of the Australian Aborigines.]
Universität Wien, 1950. Phil.Fak.Diss. 153, 3, 4, 2, 11, 10pp. maps, tbls.

DRYBURGH, Irene M.
Social change and the Australian Aborigines.
University of Western Australian, 1970. B.A. viii, 73, 6pp.

DUFALL, Barry Horace
The consumption of alcohol and the implications involved with specific reference to the Aborigines of central Australia.
Education Department of Western Australia, Teacher's Higher Certificate thesis, 1971. 81pp.

DUNCAN, Alan Towers
A survey of the education of Aborigines in New South Wales, with particular reference to its historical context.
University of Sydney, 1969. M.Ed. 644pp. figs., map, tbls.

DUNNE, Joseph Patrick
Investigation into the coloured children's backwardness in primary school subjects at three metropolitan schools in Perth, Western Australia.
University of Western Australia, 1958. B.Ed.
This thesis is missing from the collection of the Faculty of Education of the University of Western Australia.

DUNTON, Jennifer M.
Aspects of relations between colonists and Aborigines in New South Wales from 1788-1838 (with special reference to the *Sydney Gazette* from 1803).
University of New England, 1969. B.A. (Hons.). 123pp. illus.

DUTTON, Thomas Edward
Some phonological aspects of Palm Island Aboriginal English: a study of the free conversational speech of four Aboriginal children at Palm Island Aboriginal settlement in North Queensland.
University of Queensland, 1964. M.A. qualifying essay. xxiv, 549pp. diags., figs.

The informal speech of Palm Island Aboriginal children, north Queensland: a study of the structure of the conversational English of Aboriginal children aged from nine to fourteen years on Palm Island, and a comparison of the structure with that of Aboriginal English of similar informants elsewhere.
University of Queensland, 1966, M.A. xxiii, 457pp.
Publications:
'The informal English speech of Palm Island Aboriginal children', *Journal of English Linguistics*, 3, 1969, 18-36.
'Informal English in the Torres Straits' in W. S. Ramson (ed.), *English transported: essays on Australian English*. Canberra, Australian National University Press, 1970, pp.137-60.

DYKE, Lilian
Totemism and social control.
University of Western Australia, 1968. B.A. 63pp.

ECKERMANN, Anne-Katrin
Contact: an ethnographical analysis of three Aboriginal communities including a comparative and cross-cultural analysis of value orientations.
University of Queensland, 1973. M.A. 2 v. (569pp.). diags., maps, plans, pls., pls., tbls.

EDMUNDS, Mary Philomena
Culture and cognition: a study of the bilingual program of education in Aboriginal schools in the Northern Territory.
University of Queensland, 1975. B.A. (Hons.). iv, 91pp. diags., maps, tbls.

EDWARDS, Daphne
The development of 'self-conscious' part-Aboriginal communities: with special reference to metropolitan areas.
  University of Western Australia, 1969. B.A. 48pp.

EDWARDS, Neil R.
Native education in the Northern Territory of Australia: a critical account of its aims, development and present position.
  University of Fydney, 1962. M.Ed. xi, 355pp. map, pls.

EGGLESTON, Elizabeth Moulton
Aborigines and the administration of justice: a critical analysis of the application of criminal law to Aborigines.
  Monash University, 1970. PhD. xiv, 595pp. map, tbls.

EGGLESTON, Helga, J.
A history of the Drysdale River Mission.
  Claremont Teachers' College, 1966. History thesis. iii, 24, [1]pp.

ELIAS, Gordon C.
Socio-linguistics: a classroom revisited.
  University of Queensland, 1976. M.Ed. Studies. 78pp.

ELLIS, Catherine J.
Aboriginal music making: a study of central Australian music.
  University of Glasgow, 1961. Ph.D. 368pp. catalogue of rhythms, charts, figs., music, tbls.

ELLIS, Mancel Rose
Values and ethnic attitude: a multi-dimensional study.
  University of Queensland, 1962. B.A.(Hons.). v, 38pp. pls., tbls.

ELLIS, Robert William
A historical geography of the pre-European inhabitants of the Adelaide Plains.
  University of Adelaide, 1968. B.A.(Hons.). viii, 90pp. pls., tbls.

EMERSON, Penelope L.
Hooka Point: a disturbed site.
  University of Sydney, 1973. (B.A.(Hons.). 31pp. figs., tbls.

EVANS, Gaynor
Thursday Island, 1878-1914.
  University of Queensland, 1972. B.A.(Hons.). 180pp.

EVANS, Kay Elizabeth
Missionary efforts towards Cape York Aborigines 1886-1910: a study of culture contact.
University of Queensland, 1969. B.A. (Hons.). iii, 106, [12]pp. pls., tbls.

EVANS, Raymond L.
European-Aboriginal relations in Queensland 1880-1910: a chapter of contact.
University of Queensland, 1965. B.A. (Hons.). iv, 309pp.

FALKENBERG, Johannes
Kin and totem relations of Australian Aborigines in the Port Keats district.
Universitetet i Oslo, 1962. Ph.D. 271pp. diags., maps, tbls.
Publication:
Kin and totem: group relations of Australian Aborigines in the Port Keats district. Oslo, Oslo University Press, 1962. 271pp. maps, diags., tbls., bibliog. Also published as Bulletin No. 9, Universitetet Ethnografiske Museum, University of Oslo.

FARMER, Richard Lindsay
Commonwealth Government Aboriginal policy, 1901-1953.
Australian National University, 1966. M.A. qualifying essay. [74]pp.

FARMER, Ronald G.
The 1964 revision of the P.I.R. IV, a performance test for measuring the cognitive capacity of the indigenes of Australia and Papua-New Guinea.
University of Queensland, 1964. B.A. (Hons.). v, 33pp. diag., tbls.

FARNILL, Douglas
Aboriginal marriage arrangements: a study of the degree of rigidity with which the kinship connections prescribe social behaviour.
University of Sydney, 1964. B.A. (Hons.). 71pp. diags., tbls.

FEATHERSTONE, Guy Fontaine
The life and times of James Bonwick; part one — apostle of moral enlightenment.
University of Melbourne, 1968. M.A. vii, 220pp. illus., maps.

FENNER, Frank John
Anthropometric observations on South Australian Aborigines, etc.

Local implantation of sulphamilomide for prevention and treatment of gas gangrene in heavily contaminated wounds.
University of Adelaide, 1942. M.D. various pagings, collection of papers.

FENN LUSHER, Evadne Jean
Study of a community in Australia.
Cambridge University, 1951. M.Litt. 271pp.

FINCH, Noel G.
Torres Strait Island education: past, present and a proposal for the future re-organization of the primary school system.
University of Queensland, 1975. M.Ed. Studies. 273pp.

FINE, Michael
An analysis of adopted cults in central Australia: social groups and ritual amongst the Walbiri and Aranda.
University of Sydney, 1975. B.A. (Hons.). 60, [6]pp. diag., map.

FINK, Ruth Annette
Social stratification: a sequel to the assimilation process in a part-Aboriginal community; report of four months' field work at Brewarrina, New South Wales.
University of Sydney, 1955. M.A. 137pp. diags., pls., tbls.
Publication:
'The caste barrier — an approach to the assimilation of part-Aborigines in north west New South Wales', *Oceania*, 28 (2), 1957, 100-10.

The changing status and cultural identity of Western Australian Aborigines: a field study of Aborigines in the Murchison District, Western Australia, 1955-1957.
Columbia University, 1960. Ph.D. vii, 306pp. illus., pls, tbls.

Traditional songs bring an appendix to *The changing status and cultural identity of Western Australian Aborigines: a field study of Aborigines in the Murchison District, Western Australia, 1955-1957.*
Columbia University, 1960. Ph.D. 25pp.
Publications:
'The changing Aborigines of Western Australia', *Transactions New York Academy of Science*, 20, 1958.
'The contemporary situation of change among part-Aborigines in Western Australia' in R. M. Berndt and C. M. Berndt (eds.), *Aboriginal man in Australia.* Sydney, Angus and Robertson, 1965. pp.419-34.

'Guided social change at the community level' in M. Reay (ed.), *Aborigines now, new perspectives in the study of Aboriginal communities.* Sydney, Angus and Robertson, 1964. pp.143-50.

FISCHER-COLBRIE, Mathilde J.
Speere, Speereschleudern und Keulen der Pankala, kulturhistorische and linguistische Beziehungen.
[Spears, spear-catapults and clubs of the Parnkala. References relating to the history of civilisation and linguistics.]
Universität Wien, 1940. Phil.Fak.Diss. xxiv, 187pp. illus., maps, tbls.

FISHER, Jane R. W.
Cultural relevance of stimulus pictures as a determinant of achievement and affiliation motivation in Aboriginal and European adolescent girls.
University of Queensland, 1973. B.A. (Hons.). vii, 73pp. tbls.

FITZGERALD, Paul A.
A study of the Gerard Aboriginal Reserve community.
University of Adelaide, 1971. B.A. (Hons.). 104pp. diag., maps.

FITZPATRICK, David G.
Assimilation of Australian Aborigines.
University of Queensland, 1973. B.Sc. (Hons.). iv, 70pp. fig., tbls.

FLETCHER, Kim Francis
The nature and role of trade and exchange in traditional Aboriginal Australia.
University of Western Australia, 1968. B.A. ii, 95pp. map.

FLOOD, James Bernard
'Community' and Aboriginal education.
University of New England, 1972. B.Ed. xii, 223pp. figs., maps.

FLOOD, Josephine Mary
Archaeology of Yarar shelter.
Australian National University, 1966. M.A. 186pp. figs., illus., map, pls., tbls.

The moth-hunters. Investigations towards a prehistory of the southeastern highlands of Australia.
Australian National University, 1973. Ph.D. 2 v. (ix, 307pp.). diag., maps, plans, tbls.

FOGARTY, Phyllis W.
History of the Beagle Bay Mission, 1890-1962.
Claremont Teachers' College, 1963. History thesis. ii, 27, [2]pp.

FOGGITT, Roger H.
Some psycholinguistic factors underlying performance on a non-verbal test of intelligence for ethnically distinct groups of children.
University of Queensland, 1969. M.A. xi, 127pp. fig., tbls.

FORBY, Bryan Lawrence
Aspects of identity amongst Aboriginal people in Adelaide.
University of Adelaide, 1970, B.A. 67pp.
──────────
Social mobility amongst Aborigines in Adelaide.
University of Adelaide, 1972. B.A.(Hons.). 103pp. tbls.

FRANK, Amalie Maria
Botenstäbe und Wegzeichen in Australien.
[Messenger sticks and sign-posts in Australia.]
Universität Wien, 1940. Phil.Fak.Diss.
The Librarian, Universitätsbibliotäk Wien, reports that the university copy of this thesis is missing.

FRASER, Douglas Ferrar
Torres Strait sculpture: a study in oceanic primitive art.
Columbia University, 1959. Ph.D. 242pp. maps, pls., tbls.

FRATKIN, Elliot Mayer
The application of structural analysis of 'rites de passage', with special reference to Melanesian and Australian societies.
University of London, 1972. M.Phil. 138pp.

GALE, Fay
A study of assimilation: part Aborigines in South Australia.
University of Adelaide, 1960. Ph.D. xxii, 443pp. figs., illus., maps, tbls.
Publication:
A study of assimilation: part-Aborigines in South Australia. Adelaide, Libraries Board of South Australia, 1964. xxii, 443pp. figs., illus., maps, tbls.

GALLIMORE, Alan Jeffrey
Some factors in the susceptibility to the visual form of the Muller-

Lyer illusion, namely culture, perceptual development and pictorial depth perception.
> University of Queensland, 1972. M.Sc. (qualifying). v, 38pp. figs., tbls.

GALLOWAY, Winifred
Government and popular attitudes toward the Victorian Aborigines, 1837-1867: with special reference to William Thomas, Assistant Protector and Guardian, whose period of service extended over the time studied.
> University of Melbourne, 1962. B.A. (Hons.). 74pp.

GANNAN, Kathleen M.
A patriarch of old: Peter Beveridge and the Aborigines. Swan Hill and Tyntynder 1845-1877.
> University of Melbourne, 1971. B.A. (Hons.). 54pp. diags.

GEEVES, Richard T.
Sealers in Bass Strait to 1835.
> Australian National University, 1973. B.A. (Hons.). ii, 92pp.

GEORGE, Kenneth R. *see* **SAVARTON**, Stanislaw

GIBBS, Ronald Malcolm
Humanitarian theories and the Aboriginal inhabitants of South Australia to 1860.
> University of Adelaide, 1960. B.A. (Hons.). 125pp. illus.

GIBSON, Edward Gordon
Culture contact on Sunday Island
> University of Sydney, 1951. M.A. (Hons.). 149pp. illus., maps., tbls.

GILES, Diana
The relationship between education, social stratification and community development in Australian society.
> University of Western Australia, 1972. B.A. viii, 74pp. tbls.

GILLEN, Paul A.
Syntactic structures in Aboriginal cult rites.
> University of Sydney, 1970. B.A. (Hons.). 176, xvi pp. diags., figs., maps, tbls.

GLASS, Amee D.
The social significance of mythology in Australian Aboriginal society.
> University of Western Australia, 1959. B.A. 26pp.

GLOVER, Ian C.
The use of factor analysis for the discovery of artefact types.
　University of Sydney, 1965. B.A. 106pp.
　Publication:
'The use of factor analysis for the discovery of artefact types', *Mankind*,
　7 (1), 1969, 36-51.

GODDARD, Francis
The retardation of native children in the south-west of Western
Australia and its possible amelioration by better housing.
　University of Western Australia, 1954. B.Ed. 28pp.

GOLEBY, Alison V.
The problems and feuds engaging the attention of the settlers in the
northern districts of New South Wales, 1842-1859.
　University of Queensland, 1951. B.A. (Hons.). 45pp.

GOOD, Elizabeth
Aboriginal child health.
　University of Queensland, 1972. B.Soc. Work.
　　No copy of this thesis is held at the University of Queensland.

GOODALE, Jane Carter
The Tiwi women of Melville Island, Australia.
　University of Pennsylvania, 1959. Ph.D. xiv. 313, 1pp. diags., maps.

GOSS, Anthony R.
Anti-5 Hydroxytryptamine activity in extracts of scaevola spinescens
[and] the metabolism of dapsone in Aboriginal leprosy patients.
　University of Western Australia, 1973. M.Sc. 103pp.

GRANDOWSKI, Edwin
Lebens-Abläufe bei den Aranda (Zentral-Australien) und den
Hagenbergleuten (Neu-Guinea)
[Life of the Aranda (Central Australia) and Mt. Hagen people (New
Guinea).]
　Freie Universität, Berlin, 1956. Phil.Fak.Diss. 312pp. tbls.

GRANT, John McKenzie
Cross-cultural curriculum development with particular reference to
socio-cultural foundations and to industrial arts.
　University of New South Wales, 1971. Ph.D. viii, 477pp. diags., pls.,
　tbls.

Publications:
'The objectives of industrial arts education in secondary schools',
Industrial Arts Bulletin, 11, 1971, 56.
'Children who are different: adapting the curriculum', *Special Schools
Bulletin*, 9, 1972, 3, 10-12.
'Media matter', *Developing Education*, 1, 1973, 1, 14-17.
'The school in the community', *Developing Education*, 1, 1974, 6, 16-
21.

GRAU, Rudolf
Die Gruppenehe, ein völkerkundliches Problem.
[Group marriage, an ethnological problem.]
    Karl-Marx-Universität, Leipzig, 1931. Phil.Fak.Diss. 145pp.

GRAVE, Keith Cyril
Timing of facial growth in Australian Aborigines: a study of relations
with stature and ossification in the hand around puberty.
    University of Adelaide, 1971. M.D.S. xviii, 235pp. figs., map, pls.,
    tbls.
Publications:
with T. Brown, M. J. Barrett and K. C. Grave, 'Facial growth and
    skeletal maturation at adolescence', *Tandlaegebladet*, 75, 1211-22.
Timing of facial growth: a study of relation with stature and
    ossification in the hand around puberty', *Australian Orthodontic
    Journal*, 3, June 1973, 117-22.

GRAVES, Adrian Arthur
An anatomy of race relations: land legislation and culture clash in
South Australia, Natal and New Zealand.
    University of Adelaide, 1973. B.A. (Hons.). 180pp.

GRAY, Gavin R.
The social structure and organization of the Australian Aborigine.
    University of Western Australia, 1961. B.A. [1], 23pp.

GRAY, Jane Cameron
Annotated bibliography of material on Aborigines suitable for use in
primary/secondary school libraries.
    University of New South Wales, 1973. Dip.Lib. 56pp.
Publications:
'The image of the Aborigine in literature', *Children's Libraries
    Newsletter*, 9 (2), 1973, 35-8.
Black and white Australians, Bibliography No. 1, N.S.W. Division of
    the Library Association of Australia, School Libraries Section, 1973.

GREEN, Neville J.
The effects of alien impact on the culture of the Swan and Canning
River Aborigines from the first settlement in 1829 up to 1850.
 Education Department of Western Australia, Teacher's Higher
 Certificate thesis, 1965. 68pp.

GREENWAY, John
Anthropology in Australia.
 University of Colorado (Boulder), 1958. M.A. 101pp. map.

GRIFFITH, Robyn
A discussion of the hand motif in Australian Aboriginal art.
 University of New England, 1971. B.Litt. 160,8,[1]pp. figs., maps,
 tbls.

GUARIGLIA, Guglielmo
Prophetismus und Heilsbewegungen bei den Naturvölkern Amerikas,
Ozeaniens, Australiens und Afrikas, mit einem Anhang über Asien.
[Prophetism and healing movement with the primitive races of
America, the Pacific Islands, Australia and Africa with an appendix
about Asia.]
 Universität Wien, 1958. Phil.Fak.Diss. 369pp.
Publication:
*Prophetismus und Heilserwartungsbewegungen als völkerkundliches
und religonsgeschichtliches Problem.* Vienna, Berger, 1959.

GUTHRIE, Gerard Simon
Aboriginal   attitudes   to   migration;   Cherbourg   settlement,
Queensland.
 University of New England, 1976. M.Soc.Sci. (Hons.). xvii, 331pp.
 figs., pls., tbls.

HACKETT, Cecil John
Boomerang legs and yaws in Australian Aborigines, with a description
of bone lesions resulting from yaws.
 University of Adelaide, 1935. M.D. 2 v. (iv, 214pp.). case notes,
 illus., pls.
Publication:
'Boomerang legs and yaws in Australian Aborigines', *Transactions
 Royal Society for Tropical Medicine and Hygiene,* 30 (2), 1936, 137-
 50. Reprinted as *Monograph No. 1 of Royal Society for Tropical
 Medicine and Hygiene,* 1936.

HAGEN, Karl
Über die Music einiger Naturvölker (Australier, Melanesier, Polynesier).
[The music of several primitive races (Australian, Melanesian, Polynesian).]
Friedrich-Schiller Universität, Jena, 1892. Phil.Fak.Diss. 35pp.

HAGEN, Roderic ,
Black realities in white Australia: an analysis of Australian race relations within a framework of Berger and Luckman's Sociology of Knowledge.
Macquarie University, 1974. B.A. (Hons.). 84, [3]pp.

HAGLUND-CALLEY, Laila G. B.
The relation between the Broadbeach burials and the cultures of eastern Australia.
University of Queensland, 1968. M.A. v, 277pp. charts, diags., illus., maps, pls.

HALL, Allen Harry
A depth-study of the Thaayorr language of the Edward River tribe, Cape York Peninsula: being a description of the phonology with a brief grammatical outline and samples of lexicon and oral literature.
University of Queensland, 1968. M.A. 353pp. figs., maps, tbls.

―――
A study of the Thaayorr language of the Edward River tribe, Cape York Peninsula, Queensland, being a description of the grammar.
University of Queensland, 1972. Ph.D. 2 v (638pp.). diags., figs., illus., tbls.

HALL, John Raymond
Drinking behaviour amongst part-Aborigines in a Western Australian community.
University of Western Australia, 1965. B.A. 83pp.

HALLIWELL, Leslie Marsden
Community leadership and social welfare in a Queensland provincial city.
University of Queensland, 1964. M.Soc.St. [1], xi, 168pp. diags., tbls.

HAMILTON, Annette
Nature and nurture — child rearing in north-central Arnhem Land.
University of Sydney, 1970. M.A. [3], 193pp. maps, tbls.

HAMPTON, Tony *see* BUSBY, Frank *et al.*

HANSON, Roderick Arthur David
Economic development of the Aboriginal reserves in Australia — a short review.
    University of New England, 1971. B.Ag.Ec.[10], 130pp. maps, tbls.

HARAESSER, Albert
Rechtsverletzung und Ermittlung des Täters bei den australischen Eingeborenen.
[Crime and locating the criminal amongst the Australian Aborigines.]
    Universität Wien, 1931. Phil.Fak.Diss. 113, xxiv pp.

HARDLEY, Roger Gordon
Some of the factors that influenced the coastal, riverine and insular habitats of the Aborigines of south-east Queensland and northern New South Wales.
    University of Queensland, 1975. B.A. (Hons.). 90pp.

HARGRAVE, John C.
Leprosy in the Northern Territory of Australia, with particular reference to the Aborigines of Arnhem Land and the arid regions of the Northern Territory.
    University of Sydney, 1975. M.D. 2 v. (xiii, 397pp.). diags., illus., maps, tbls.

HARRIES, William T.
The effect of attendance at a pre-school on the level of intellectual functioning of mixed blood Aboriginal children on the mid north coast of New South Wales: an investigation using the Revised Stanford Binet Test (Form L-M) and the Illinois Test of Psycholinguistic Abilities as measures of intellectual functioning.
    University of New England, 1967. B.Litt. 238pp. diags., pls., tbls.

HARRIGAN, Neil Patrick
The prediction of commercial ability in Australian Aboriginal females.
    University of Queensland, 1971. Dip.Psych. 60pp. tbls.

HARRIS, David
The failure of the Port Phillip Protectorate (1838-1849).
    University of Melbourne, 1975. B.A. (Hons.). iv, 59p.

HARRIS, Joy Juanell Kinslow
Descriptive and comparative study of the Gunwingguan languages,
Northern Territory.
  Australian National University, 1969. Ph.D. viii, 169pp. map, tbls.

HARRISON, Brian Ward
The Myall Creek massacre and its signifance in the controversy over the
Aborigines during Australia's early squatting period.
  University of New England, 1967. B.A. (Hons.). 125pp. illus.

HARRISON, Cathleen M. A.
A study of the culture contact situation in Collie.
  University of Western Australia, 1960. B.A. (Hons.). xiv, 126pp.
  maps, pls.

HARRISON, Marelle
Towards a curriculum for values: development and evaluation of a
curriculum unit with the effective area for Aboriginal studies.
  Macquarie University, 1974. B.A. (Hons.). 367pp. illus.

HART, Arthur Maxwell
A history of the education of full-blood Aborigines in South Australia,
with references to the Northern Territory.
  University of Adelaide, 1971. M.Ed. 237pp. illus., maps.

HART, Erica Jean
An analysis of theoretical concepts in the study of Australian
Aboriginal art.
  University of Queensland, 1972. B.A. (Hons.). 70pp.

HART, Joan A.
A study of the cognitive capacity of a group of Australian Aboriginal
children.
  University of Queensland, 1965. M.A. qualifying essay. vii, 43pp.
  tbls.

HART, Philip R.
The Church of England in Tasmania under Bishop Montgomery, 1889-
1901.
  University of Tasmania, 1963. M.A. xi, 339pp. maps.

HARTWIG, Mervyn C.
The Coniston killings.
  University of Adelaide, 1960. B.A. (Hons.). 85pp. maps, pls.

The progress of white settlement in the Alice Springs district and its effects upon the Aboriginal inhabitants, 1860-1894.
> University of Adelaide, 1965. Ph.D. xxiii, 669pp. maps, tbls.

HARVEY, Alison
Ethnic and sociological study of an Australian mixed-blood group in Alice Springs, Northern Territory, with special reference to ethnic assimilation and interaction of groups.
> University of Sydney, 1946. M.A. 177pp. tbls.

HARVEY, Spencer Wallace
Social relationships among Aboriginal and white children attending a primary school in western New South Wales.
> University of New England, 1966. Dip.Ed.Admin. 106pp. pls., tbls.

HASLUCK, Paul
A study of official policy and public opinion towards the Aborigines of Western Australia from 1829-1897.
> University of Western Australia, 1940. M.A.
> This thesis cannot be traced at the University of Western Australia.

Publication:
Black Australians. A survey of native policy in Western Australia, 1829-1897. Melbourne, Melbourne University Press, 1942. 226pp. 2nd edn, 1970.

HASSELL, Kathleen Lilian
The relation between the settlers and Aborigines in South Australia.
> University of Adelaide, 1927. M.A. 226pp.

Publication:
The relations between the settlers and Aborigines in South Australia, 1836-1860. Adelaide, Libraries Board of South Australia, 1966. 222pp. bibliog.

HAUDE, Detlev Konrad Hendrik
Das geistige Eigentum bei den Australiern.
[The spirtual heritage of the Australian Aborigines.]
> Rheinische Friedrich-Wilhelms-Universität, Bonn, 1970. Phil.Fak. Diss. 99pp.

HAUSFELD, Russell Gordon
Aspects of Aboriginal station management, Woodenbong.
> University of Sydney, 1960. M.A. iv, 159pp. genealogical table, map.

Publication:
'Life on a typical Aboriginal station in New South Wales' in *Proceedings of Conference on New South Wales Aborigines*. Adult Education Department, University of New England, Armidale, 1959.

Value orientations: change and stress.
University of Sydney, 1972. Ph.D. 2 v. (viii, 666pp.). figs., tbls.
Publication:
'The social prediction of self-perceived mobidity', *Medical Journal of Australia*, 2, 1973, 975-8.

HAWKE, Elizabeth Natalie
Archaeological resource management: a legal perspective.
Australian National University, 1975. B.A. (Hons.). 84pp. pls.

HEALY, John Joseph
The treatment of the Aborigine in Australian literature from the beginning to the present day.
University of Texas at Austin, 1968. Ph.D. 403pp.
Publications:
'The convict and the Aborigine: the quest for freedom in "Ralph Rushleigh" ', *Australian Literary Studies*, 3 (4), 1968, 243-53.
'The treatment of the Aborigine in early Australian fiction', *Australian Literary Studies*, 5 (3), 1972, 233-53.

HELLSBUSCH, Sigrid
Einfluss der Jagd auf die Lebensformen der Australier.
[The influence of hunting on the life forms of the Australian Aborigines.]
Friedrich-Wilhelms-Universität, Berlin, 1941. Phil.Fak.Diss. 227pp.
Publication:
Einfluss der Jagd auf die Lebensform der Australier. Berlin, Ebering, 1941. 227pp.

HENDERSON, Margaret Helen
A preliminary investigation into some of the socialization processes operating within the families of part-Aborigines in the urban situation in Western Australia.
University of Western Australia, 1965. B.A. i, 71pp. tbls.

HENWOOD, Beverly
A theoretical consideration of the relevance of community social work in an Aboriginal setting.
University of New South Wales, 1968. B.Soc. Work (Hons.). 60pp.

HERBERT, Alfred G.
The advantages and disadvantages of both segregation and assimilation in the process of integrating the Australian native.
Education Department of Western Australia, Teacher's Higher Certificate thesis, 1960. 68pp.

HERCUS, Luise A.
Studies on Middle Indo-Iranian and Australian Aboriginal languages.
Australian National University, 1976. Ph.D. various pagings. Published works.

HESS, Felix
Boomerangs, aerodynamics and motion.
Rijksuniversiteit te Groningen, 1975. Phil.Fak.Diss. 555pp. diags., illus., pls., tbls.

HETHERINGTON, William Raymond
Aboriginal policy in South Australia.
University of Sydney, 1946. M.A.
This thesis was accepted at the University of Sydney, but no copies can now be located.

HIATT, Betty
Some aspects of the economy of the Tasmanian Aborigines.
University of Sydney, 1965. B.A. 133, xv pp. maps, pls., tbls.

HIATT, Lester Richard
An analysis of conflict in some areas of Aboriginal Australia.
University of Sydney, 1957. B.A. unpaged, map.
_____
Conflict in northern Arnhem Land
Australian National University, 1962. Ph.D. vii, 177pp. diags., map.
Publication;
Kinship and conflict. Brisbane, Jacaranda Press 1965 xv, 169pp. figs., maps, tbls

HICKEY, Barry
The development of Catholic welfare services in Western Australia.
University of Western Australia 1971. M. Soc. Work. 193pp.

HILL, Ivor W.
Australian Aboriginal stone tool terminology and the ethnographic evidence.
University of Queensland, 1976. B.A. (Hons.). 170pp.

HILLIKER, Jeffrey Lorne
The politics of impoverishment: a history of Aboriginal wage policy in
the Northern Territory of Australia.
University of Sydney, 1976. M.A. [iv], 183pp.

HILLMAN, Margery
The development of racial attitudes in young children with reference to
the Australian Aboriginal.
University of Western Australia, 1946. B.A. 140pp. diags., illus.,
tbls.

HINTON, Peter D.
The prosperous Aborigines: the industrialization of a mission
community.
University of Sydney, 1966. M.A. 210pp. maps, pls., tbls.

HOCKING, Barbara Joyce
Aboriginal land rights — the political significance of the relationship
between historical white situations in Australia and white Australian
Aboriginal policies.
Monash University, 1974. M.A. preliminary essay. 134pp.
_____
Native land rights.
Monash University, 1971. LL.M. 280pp.

HOFFMAN, David Charles
In place of shanties.
University of Queensland, 1966. B.Arch. various pagings, illus.

HOFFMAN, Trevor David
The status of Australian Aboriginal land rights following *Milirrpum v.
Nabalco P.L. and the Commonwealth of Australia.* (1970) 17 F.L.R.
141.
University of Western Australia, 1976. B. Juris. 101pp.

HOGAN, Peggy
The part-Aborigines: problems of adjustment as a minority group.
University of Western Australia, 1964. B.Sc. iv, 53pp.

HOLM, Neil
Future time perspective in children from three Northern Territory
Aboriginal communities.
University of New England, 1971. B.A. (Hons.). ix, 147pp. figs.,
tbls.

HOPE, Geoffrey Scotford
Pollen studies at Wilson's Promontory, Victoria.
  University of Melbourne, 1968. M.Sc. viii, 289pp. figs., maps, pls., tbls.

HOPE, Jeannette Helen
Biogeography of the mammals of the islands of Bass Strait, with an account of variation in the genus *potorus*.
  Monash University, 1969. Ph.D. xi, 338pp. figs., illus., maps., pls.

HORMANN, Bernard L.
Extinction and survival: a study of the reaction of Aboriginal populations to European expansions.
  University of Chicago, 1950. Ph.D. 444pp.
Publication:
'Rigidity and fluidity in race relations' in A. W. Lind (ed.), *Race relations in world perspective*. Honolulu, University of Hawaii Press, 1956. pp.25-48.

HOSKINS, Graham
The Aboriginal reserves in Queensland, 1871-1885, and the movement to ameliorate and improve the conditions of the Aborigines, 1870-1879.
  University of Queensland, 1967. B.A. (Hons.). 272pp.

HOWARD, Michael C.
Nyoongah politics: Aboriginal politics in the south-west of Western Australia.
  University of Western Australia, 1975. Ph.D. [i], 215pp. maps.

HOWE, David G. L.
Aerodynamics of boomerangs.
  City of Leicester College of Education, Leicester, 1972. Thesis (education). 47pp. diags.

HOWELL, Bette M.
Culture contact: a study of the Australian Aboriginal and his reaction and adjustment to the Australian-European way of life.
  University of Western Australia, 1964. B.A. 35pp.

HUGHES, Thomas B.
The material culture of the Tasmanian Aborigines and its relationship to that of Australia.
  University of New Mexico, 1954. M.A. v, 247pp. charts, diags., maps, pls.

HUME, Stuart H. R.
The analysis of a stone assemblage to determine change.
University of Sydney, 1965. B.A.(Hons.). 92pp. diags., figs., pls., tbls.

HUNT, Jennifer Mary
Schools for Aboriginal children in the Adelaide district, 1836-1852.
University of Adelaide, 1971. B.A.(Hons.). 74pp.

HUNTSMAN, Robert William
The attainments, aspirations and attitudes of part-Aboriginal school children.
University of New England 1966. M.A. 391pp.

HYE-KERDAL, Kathe
Die kulturgeschichliche Bedeutung des Tike-Spieles in der Südsee.
[The meaning relating to the history of civilization of the tika-play in the Pacific.]
Universität Wien, 1952. Phil.Fak.Diss. xivi, 221, 151pp.

IREDALE, Robin R.
The enigma of assimilation: the position of the part-Aboriginal in New South Wales.
University of Sydney, 1965. B.A.(Hons.). 200pp. graphs, maps., pls., tbls.

JACKES, Mary K.
Licence and alliance: a study of joking relationships in three primitive societies.
University of New England, 1957. iii, 288pp. figs., maps.

JENKINS, Graham
The Aborigines' Friends Association and the Ngarrindjeri people.
University of Adelaide, 1976. M.A. 2 v. (xxiv, 512pp.). map, pls.

JENNER, John D.
Dental development in Australian Aborigines: a study of relations with growth and skeletal maturity around adolescence.
University of Adelaide, 1972. M.D.S. ix, 163pp. figs., tbls.

JENNETT, Christine
Thesis report investigating the influence of the degree of contact with Aborigines on the negative or positive attitudes of white people towards

them. A study conducted at Moree, in north-western New South Wales.
University of New South Wales, 1966. B.A. iii, 35, xvii pp. tbls.

Racism and the rise of black power in Australia.
University of New England, 1970. M.A. qualifying essay. 54, [29]pp. tbls.

JEPSON, Rodney John
The social and cultural factors affecting Aboriginal school performance in Walgett.
University of New England, 1971. B.Litt. v, 119pp. tbls., figs., diags.

JOHANSONS, Kurt
Aboriginal settlements and housing in the Northern Territory.
University of Queensland, 1966. B.Arch. 121pp. diags., maps, pls.

JOHNSTON, Susan Lindsay
The New South Wales government policy towards Aborigines, 1880-1909.
University of Sydney, 1970. M.A. [7], xviii, xix, 175pp. tbls.

JOLLES, Anna
Erziehung bei den Australiern. Eine Untersuchung über die ersten Anfangs und Entstehungsgründe der Erziehung.
[The child-rearing practices of the Australian Aborigines. An examination of meaning of child-rearing practices.]
Universität Wien, 1919. Phil.Fak.Diss.
The Librarian, Universitätbibliotek Wien reports that the university copy of this thesis is missing.

JONES, Dorothy Lilian Nay
The treatment of the Aborigine in Australian fiction.
University of Adelaide, 1960. M.A. v, 107pp.

JONES, Hector Gordon
Part 1. The dentition and palate of Australian fossil man.
Part 2. The general search for primitive features.
University of Sydney, 1940. D.D.S. 159pp. figs., pls., tbls.

JONES, Rhys
Rocky Cape and the problem of the Tasmanians.
University of Sydney, 1971. Ph.D. 631, 126pp. diags., maps, pls., tbls.

JONES, Trevor A.
An introductory survey of the Aboriginal music of Arnhem Land.
    University of Sydney, 1953. B.A. (Hons.). 104pp. map, music, pls.

———
Arnhem Land music (north Australia).
    University of Sydney, 1958. M.A.(Hons.). 174pp. 174 music
    examples, 30 full translations.
Publications:
'Arnhem Land music. Pt.2. A musical survey', *Oceania*, 26(4), 1956,
    252-339; 28(1), 1957, 1-30.
Above articles subsequently republished as A. P. Elkin and T. A. Jones,
    Arnhem Land music (north Australia). Oceania Monograph No. 9,
    1958.

KABERRY, Phyllis Mary
The position of women in an Australian Aboriginal society.
    University of London. 1938. Ph.D. viii, 481pp.
Publication:
Aboriginal woman — sacred and profane. London, G. Routledge &
    Sons, 1939. xxxi, 294pp. illus.

KABO, Vladimir Rafaelovich
Origin and early history of the Aborigines of Australia.
    Moscow M. V. Lomonosov State University, 1969. Ph.D. 408pp.

KAMIEN, Max
The doctor as an agent of change. An action oriented epidemiological
and sociological study of the health of a rural Aboriginal community.
    University of New South Wales, 1975. M.D. 2 v. (iv, 443, 31,
    10pp.). figs., tbls.
Publications:
'Vitamin and nutritional status of a part Aboriginal community',
    Australian and New Zealand Journal of Medicine, 4, 1974, 126-37.
with John A. Bissett, 'The future role of the District Hospital in rural
    Australia', *National Hospital*, 18(6), 1974, 21-4.

KAMMINGA, Johan
Microscopic and experimental study of Australian Aboriginal stone
tools.
    University of Sydney, 1971. B.A. (Hons.). 173pp. figs., illus., maps,
    pls., tbls.

KARATHANASIS, Charalambos
The intelligence of Western Australian Aboriginal children.
    University of Western Australia, 1969. M.Psych. vi, 80pp. tbls.

KEARNEY, George E.
P.I.R. IV : a performance test for indigenous peoples.
University of Queensland, 1962. B.Com. v, 53pp. figs., tbls.

——— Some aspects of the general cognitive ability of various groups of Aboriginal Australians as assessed by the Queensland Test.
University of Queensland, 1966. Ph.D. xix, 479pp. figs., illus., maps, tbls.

KEATS, Bronya Joy Beveridge
Genetic aspects of growth and population structure in indigenous peoples of Australia and New Guinea.
Australian National University, 1976. Ph.D. 189pp. figs., maps, tbls.

KEEN, Sandra L.
A description of the Yukulta language — an Australian Aboriginal language of north-west Queensland.
Monash University, 1972. M.A. 298pp. map.

KEITER, Friedrich
Studien an australischen und melanesischen Unterkiefern aus dem Nachlasse Pöchs.
[Studies of the Australian and Melanesian lower jaw, from Poch's collection.]
Universität Wien, 1928. Phil.Fak.Diss. 136pp.

KELLOCK, Wendy Lorraine
Studies on minor non-metrical skeletal variants in the mouse and man.
University of Melbourne, 1970. M.Sc. collected papers.

KELLY, Alexandra
The Australian spearthrower.
University of Sydney, 1970. B.A. (Hons.). 170pp. illus., maps.

KENNEDY, Nannette
Culture, personality and adjustment: implications for Aboriginal school children.
Flinders University, 1971. B.A. (Hons.). v, 75, 18pp.

KERSHAW, Helen
A study and an annotated representative bibliography of children's fiction about Aborigines and legends.
University of New South Wales, 1970. Dip.Lib. 90pp.

KEWAL, Helen Mary
Aboriginal children in institutions in Adelaide.
Western Teachers College, Adelaide, 1972. Advanced Diploma.
[9], 268, [2]pp. figs., pls., tbls.

KIDSON, Cheviot Stanislaus de Vere
Genetics of human populations: studies in Melanesia, Micronesia and Australia.
University of Sydney, 1968. M.D. 191pp. tbls.

KILHAM, Christine Anne
Thematic organization of Wik-Munkan discourse.
Australian National University, 1976. Ph.D. xxiii, 331pp. map.

KILKELLY, Esther N.
To-morrow, and to-morrow and to-morrow . . . : race relations in New South Wales, with special reference to a coastal Aboriginal community.
University of Auckland, 1966. xi, 339, [10]pp. maps, tbl.

KILLINGTON, Gary
Similar yet distinctive — Aborigines in urban settings, with particular reference to Adelaide.
University of Adelaide, 1973. B.A. (Hons.). [4], 193pp. tbls.

KING, Richard S.
Native welfare in the Kimberleys.
Education Department of Western Australia, Teacher's Higher Certificate thesis, 1958. 79pp.

KING-BOYES, Margaret Jessica Esmee
Substance and shadow: an examination of Aboriginal disposal practices and the mythology, philosophy, visual and aural art associated with death in the regions bounded by 20 to 39 degrees latitude South and 128 to 153 degrees longitude East.
Flinders University, 1973. M.A. 2v. (ix, 468; [95] pp.). diags., maps.

KIRKE, David Kerry
Aboriginal infant and toddler mortality and morbidity in Central Australia.
University of Adelaide, 1970. M.D. x, 149pp. figs., illus., maps, tbls.

KITSON, George E.
Native employment in the State of Western Australia: an assessment of native employment in relation to their assimilation.
University of Western Australia, 1965. B.A. v, 41pp. map, tbls.

KLEM, Marilyn J.
A study of race relations in Port Augusta.
University of Adelaide, 1973. B.A. (Hons.). 58pp. diags, maps.

KNAPMAN, Claudia Gresham
Not just another kindergarten: characteristics of participation in a pre-school for part-Aboriginal mothers and children in Adelaide.
Australian National University, 1973. M.A. [3], 131pp. tbls.

KNOWLES, Nathaniel
Totemism in Australia.
University of Pennsylvania, 1936. M.A. 40pp. maps.
Publication:
Australian cult totemism. Publications, Philadelphia Anthropological Society, I, 1939.

KNOX, Stephanie H. L.
The spatial distribution of Aborigines in New South Wales: problems of data collection and assessment within the context of government policies and public attitudes.
University of Sydney, 1972. B.A. (Hons.). 134pp. figs., maps, tbls.

KOK, Marie
The problem of Aboriginal cultural identity and its implications for all Australian children.
University of New England, 1972. B.A. (Hons.). 156pp. tbls.

KOMMERS, Jean H. M.
Protogomena tot een psychologisch anthropologische studie van de Australische Aborigines.
[A psychological-anthropological study of the Australian Aborigines.]
Katholieke Universiteit, Nijmegen, 1972, M.A. 82pp.

KOTZ, Alfred
Über die astronomischen Kenntnisse der Naturvölker Australiens und der Südsee.

[The knowledge of astronomy of the primitive races of Australia and the South Seas.]
Karl-Marx-Universität, Leipzig, 1911. Phil.Fak.Diss. 69pp.

KRASTINS, Valda
The Tiwi: a cultural history of the Australian Aborigines on Bathurst and Melville Islands, 1705-1942.
Australian National University, 1972. B.A. (Hons.). iv, 83pp. maps, pls.

KRUEGER-KELMAR, John
Beiträge zur vergleichenden Ethnologie und Anthropologie der Neuholländer, Polynesier und Melanesier.
[A contribution to the comparison of the ethnology and anthropology of the Australian, Polynesian and Melanesian.]
Georg-August Universität zu Göttingen, 1905. Phil.Fak.Diss. 51pp.

KUPKA, Karel
Anonymat de l'artiste primitif, pientre d'écorces en Australie.
[The primitive artist: bark paintings in Australia.]
Université de Paris, 1968. Thèse doctorat en ethnologie. 2v. (513pp.). pls. [Publication de la Société des Océanistes, No. 24.]

KUUSK, Sven
Deciduous tooth crown morphology in a tribe of Australian Aborigines: a study of twelve non-metric traits.
University of Adelaide, 1973. M.D.S. 157pp. figs., illus., tbls.

LAI, Lawrence Yook Chee
Studies of inherited differences in serum proteins.
University of Western Australia, 1962. Ph.D. xiii, 240pp. pls., tbls.

LA JEUNESSE, Roger Marks
The genetic demography of the Bass Strait Island population (1815-1970).
Washington State University, 1974. Ph.D. 162pp.

LANE, Kevin H.
The Nambucca Aborigines at the time of the first white settlement: a study of their adaptation to an environment, as revealed by ethnohistorical sources.
University of New England, 1970. B.A. (Hons.). 118pp. maps, pls.

LANQUIST, Rona
Similarities in the experiences of traditional Australian Aboriginal
clevermen and of a Yaqui Indian sorcerer's apprentice.
University of Western australia, 1973. B.A. iii, 62pp.

LARSEN, Lynn
Race and spatial form: with special reference to the assimilation and
dispersal of Aborigines in the Sydney area.
Macquarie University, 1973. B.A. (Hons.). 116pp. map.

LATHBURY, Walter
Aboriginal religion: a comparative study of two myths.
University of Western Australia, 1970. B.A. 35pp.

LAUER, Brian
The Society of Friends in Queensland, 1861-1960's.
University of Queensland, 1967. B.A. (Hons.). [5], 183, [6]pp.

LAWN, Margaret Susan
Missionary influence, positive or negative? A tentative evaluation of the
effects of mission contact on the Australian Aborigines of the Arnhem
Land and Groote Eylandt reserves.
University of Western Australia, 1963. B.A. 44pp. map, tbls.

LAWRENCE, Roger
Aboriginal habitat and economy.
Australian National University, 1969. M.A. vii, 290pp. figs., maps,
tbls.
Publication:
Aboriginal habitat and economy. Canberra, Department of
Geography, School of General Studies, Australian National Univer-
sity, 1969. (Occasional Paper 6) vii, 290pp. figs., maps, tbls.

LAYTON, Robert
Myth and society in Aboriginal Arnhem Land.
University of London, 1968. M.Phil. 233pp. diags., map.
Publication:
'Myth as language in Aboriginal Arnhem Land', *Man* (n.s.), 5, 1970,
483-97.

LEATCH, May
Co-operation — competition: the cross-cultural application of a concept
of relative deprivation.
University of Queensland, 1973. Dip.Psych. vi, 53pp. illus., maps,
tbls.

LEMAIRE, James Esk
The application of some aspects of European law to the Aboriginal natives of Central Australia.
University of Sydney, 1972. LL.M. ix, 219pp.

LENDON, Guy Austin
The anatomy of the sympathetic nervous system of the Australian Aboriginal.
University of Adelaide, 1922. M.D. 46pp. diags.

LENOCH, Johann E. J.
Wurfholz and Bumerang.
[The club and the boomerang.]
Universität Wien, 1949. Phil.Fak.Diss. iii, 187, xxvii, xi, xxxi pp. pls.

LESTER, Geoffrey Standish
Aboriginal land rights: Mr Justice Blackburn and the doctrine of communal native title.
University of Melbourne, 1971. LL.B. (Hons.). iv, 150, 38pp.

LE SUEUR, Geoffrey
Housing for Aborigines in New South Wales.
University of New South Wales, 1970. B.Arch. [12], 98pp. map, plans, pls.

LICKISS, Jean Norelle
The Aboriginal people of Sydney, with special reference to the health of their children: a study in human ecology.
University of Sydney, 1971. M.D. ix, 262pp. map, pls., tbls.
Publications:
'Health problems of Sydney Aboriginal children', *Medical Journal of Australia*, 2, 1970, 995-1000.
'Aboriginal children in Sydney: the socio-economic environment', *Oceania*, 41, 1971, 201-28.
'Social deviance in Aboriginal boys', *Medical Journal of Australia*, 2, 1971, 460-70.
'Health of urban Aboriginal children: a problem for diagnosis and therapy', (Abstract), *Proceedings of the Australian Society for Medical Research*, 2, 1971, 437.
'Australian Aborigines: sociocultural factors in the urban situation', *Proceedings Seminar on Aboriginal Health Services*, Monash University Centre for Research into Aboriginal Affairs, Melbourne, May 1972.

LINDSTROM, Deanne
Some perceptual aspects of Aboriginal education.
University of Sydney, 1965. M.A. 177pp. illus., pls., tbls.

LITTLEWOOD, Robert Allen
An analysis of inbreeding and effective breeding size in the Tasmanian
hybrid population of Bass Strait.
University of California (Los Angeles), 1962. Ph.D. 121pp. diags.,
tbls.

LOCKLEY, Barbara Jean
Queensland native policy.
University of Queensland, 1957. B.A. 83pp.

LONG, Terrence
Aboriginal Australians: a summary of theories and evidence concerning
their early prehistory and origins.
University of Western Australia, 1976. B.A. 53pp.

LOOS, Noel Anthony
Frontier conflict in the Bowen district, 1861-1874.
James Cook University, 1970. M.A. qualifying essay. v, 277pp. illus.,
maps.

Aboriginal-European relations in north Queensland, 1861-1897.
James Cook University of North Queensland, 1976. Ph.D. 2 v. (viii,
863pp.). maps, pls., tbls.

LOURANDOS, Harry
Coast and hinterland: the archaeological sites of eastern Tasmania.
Australian National University, 1970. M.A. xiii, 123pp. figs., maps,
pls., tbls]

LOVE, James Robert Beattie
The grammatical structure of the Worora language of north-western
Australia.
University of Adelaide, 1932. M.A. 110, 4pp.
Publication:
An outline of Worora grammar. Sydney, 1938. Oceania Monograph
No. 3, 112-24.

LOVEJOY, Frances H.
Housing for Aborigines.
University of New England, 1974. M.Ag.Ec. v, 261pp. map, tbls.

Publication:
'Costing the Aboriginal housing problem', *Australian Quarterly*, 43 (1), 1971, 79-90.

LOVEROCK, Jennifer
The present situation of the Aboriginal Australian.
    University of Western Australia, B.A. (Hons.). 1968. 63pp.

LOWREY, Gwenyth Jill
Yirrkala 1952-53: a preliminary survey of field recordings of Australian Aboriginal music, collected by Richard A. Waterman.
    Monash University, 1972. M.A. preliminary essay. 133pp. includes lists of recordings.

LUCICH, Peter
The development of Omaha kinship terminologies in three Australian Aboriginal tribes of the Kimberley Division, Western Australia.
    University of Western Australia, 1967. M.Sc. xiv, 275pp. figs., maps, tbls.
Publication:
The development of Omaha kinship terminologies in three Australian tribes of the Kimberley Division, Western Australia. Canberra, Australian Institute of Aboriginal Studies, 1968. (Australian Aboriginal Studies No. 15, Social Anthropology Series No. 2) 275pp. figs., maps, tbls.

McBRYDE, Isabel
An archaeological survey of the New England region of New South Wales.
    University of New England, 1966. Ph.D. [7], 476pp. diags., pls. tbls.
Publication:
Aboriginal prehistory in New England: an archeological survey of northeastern New South Wales. Sydney, Sydney University Press, 1974. 400pp. figs., pls., tbls., bibliog.

McCARDELL, Anthony
Tabi songs of the Pilbara: a musical survey.
    University of Western Australia, 1970. B.A. (Hons.). ii, 80pp. illus. music, tbls.

McCARTHY, Frederick David
The material culture of eastern Australia: a study of factors entering into its composition.

University of Sydney, 1935. Dip.Anthrop. 140pp. diags., map.

Publications:

'Trade in Aboriginal Australia and trade relationships with Torres Strait, New Guinea and Malaya', *Oceania*, 9 (4), 1939, 405-38; 10 (1), 1940, 80-104; 10 (2), 1940, 171-95.

'Australian Aboriginal material culture: causative factors in its composition', *Mankind*, 2 (8), 1940, 241-69; 2 (9), 1940.

McCOOKE, Annabel Helen
Aboriginal health problems.
University of Western Australia, 1965. B.A. 40pp. tbls.

McDONNELL, Reginald Thomas
The education of the Australian Aboriginal in Queensland.
University of Queensland, 1948. B.Ed. iii, [4], 87pp. illus., map, tbls.

McEVEDY, Rosanna
New Zealand and Australian bilingual education: a comparison.
University of Western Australia, 1973. B.A. 56pp. tbls.

MACINTOSH, Neil William George
Anthropological study, Part 1. Human grouping and the background of prehistoric man. Part 2. Critical studies of the antiquity of man in Australia. In addition some facts relating to the possible origin, migration and affinities of the Australians and Tasmanians.
University of Sydney, 1950. Dip. Anthrop. Part 1: vi, 80pp. Part 2: 260pp. pls.

McKAY, Graham Richard
Rembarnga: a language of central Arnhem Land.
Australian National University, 1975. Ph.D. xvii, 405pp. tbls.

McKEICH, Robert
An examination of the acculturation, adjustment and assimilation of rural minority groups in the wider community of Western-European type societies, with particular reference to the Katukutu Aboriginal Young Men's Hostel in Perth, Western Australia, and a United Maori Mission in Auckland, New Zealand.
University of Western Australia, 1961. B.A. (Hons.). ii, 84pp.

Problems of part-Aboriginal education, with special reference to the south-west region of Western Australia.
University of Western Australia, 1971. Ph.D. xx, 623pp. diags., figs., map, tbls.

MACKNIGHT, Campbell C.
The Macassans: a study of the early trepang industry along the Northern Territory coast.
Australian National University, 1969. Ph.D. 2 v. (unpaged), 1 case. diags., maps, pls., tbls.
Publication:
'Macassans and Aborigines', *Oceania*, 42, 1972, 283-321.
The voyage to Marege': Macassan trepangers in northern Australia. Melbourne, Melbourne University Press, 1976. ix, 175pp, figs., maps, pls.

McLEAN, Gillian F.
The role of the mother among the Australian Aborigines.
University of Western Australia, 1968. B.Sc. ii, 49pp.

McMAH, Lesley A.
Quantitative analysis of the Aboriginal rock carvings in the districts of Sydney and Hawkesbury River.
University of Sydney, 1966. B.A. 152pp. figs., illus., map, tbls.

McMATH, Robert David
Problems of employment and assimilation among part-Aborigines in the Brockton area of Western Australia.
University of Western Australia, 1962. B.A. (Hons.). viii, 122pp. maps.

McNULTY, Edward Conroy
Growth, changes in the face: a semilongitudinal cephalometric study of the Australian Aboriginal by means of a co-ordinate analysis.
University of Adelaide, 1968. M.D.S. xv, 194pp. diag., illus., tbls.

McPHEAT, W. Scott
The life and work of John Flynn.
University of Queensland, 1964. Ph.D. 460pp. maps.

MADDOCK, Kenneth James
The Jabuduruwa: a study of the structure of rite and myth in an Australian Aboriginal religious cult on the Beswick Reserve, Northern Territory.
University of Sydney, 1969. Ph.D. x, 318pp. diags., maps.

MAKIN, Clarence Frank
A socio-economic anthropological survey of people of Aboriginal descent in the metropolitan region of Perth.

University of Western Australia, 1970. Ph.D. 2 v. (xiv, 541pp.). illus., maps.

MALINOWSKI, Bronislaw G.
The family among the Australian Aborigines: a sociological study. v-xv, 1-326pp.
The natives of Mailu: preliminary results of the Robert Mond research work in British New Guinea. 494-706pp. with 17 plates. (From *Transactions of the Royal Society of Southern Australia*, 39, 1915). University of London, 1916. D.Sc.

MALOT, Roger
Aboriginal dreams.
University of Western Australia, 1964. B.A. v, 120pp. figs., tbls.

MANN, Richard William King
Aboriginal housing in Western Australia, 1948-1970: a contextual study.
University of Western Australia, 1971. B.Arch. 216pp. graphs, illus., plans, pls.

MARANTA, Barry D.
Attitudes of students towards Asians and Aborigines.
University of Queensland, 1970. B.A. (Hons.). 157pp. tbl.

MACARD, Patricia
The Aborigines in Victoria, 1858-1884.
University of Melbourne, 1964. B.A. (Hons.). 79pp.
Publication:
'Early Victoria and the Aborigines', *Melbourne Historical Journal*, 4, 1964, 23-9.

MARCHANT, Leslie R.
Native administration in Western Australia, 1886-1905
University of Western Australia, 1954. B.A. (Hons.). 125pp. pls., tbls.

MARKS, Stewart Raglan
A study of mission policy in Western Australia, 1846-1959, being a study of ten representative missions.
University of Western Australia, 1959. B.A. (Hons.).
This thesis cannot be located at the University of Western Australia.
Publication:
'Mission policy in Western Australia, 1846-1959', *University Studies in Western Australian History*, 3 (4), 1960, 60-106.

MARKUS, Andrew
The burden of hate: the Australian inter-racial experience, 1880-1901. A comparative study of the Australian mainland colonies and California, with special emphasis on the working class.
La Trobe University, 1975, Ph.D. 2 v. (xiii, 590pp.).

MARTIN, Marilynn Kay
The Australian band: a diachronic model of post-contact change.
State University of New York at Buffalo, 1970. Ph.D. 265pp.

MARTYN, Marjorie Joyce
The influence of geographical environment on the development of a rural population — Murwillumbah, Tweed River.
University of Sydney, 1947. M.A. 142pp. figs., maps, pls., tbls.

MARUN, Ljubomir Hrvoje
The Mirning and their predecessors on the coastal Nullabor Plain.
University of Sydney, 1974. Ph.D. 2 v. (353; 3, 4 pp.). diags., pls., tbls.

MASSEY, David Ross
Locus of control and value orientations: a cross-cultural study.
University of Queensland, 1974. Dip. Psych. vii, 79pp. tbls.

MAZENGARB, Kathleen
Kinship recognition, geographical mobility and family structure among Aborigines and part-Aborigines in Australia.
University of Sydney, 1967. B.A. (Hons.). xiii, 93pp. diags., maps.

MEAGHER, Sara J.
Tjurunga and their relation to Aboriginal life.
University of Western Australia, 1960. B.A. 25pp.

A reconstruction of the traditional life of the Aborigines of the southwest of Western Australia.
University of Western Australia, 1976. M.A. 2 v. (615pp.).

MEEHAN, Betty Frances
The form, distribution and antiquity of Australian Aboriginal mortuary practices, being a study of their material culture and the manner in which they utilised their physical environment.
University of Sydney, 1971. M.A. 2 v. (viii, 281pp., vol. 2 unpaged). maps, pls., tbls.

Shell bed to shell midden.
  Australian National University, 1976. Ph.D. 2 v. (vii, 252; [99]pp.). diags., maps, pls., tbls.

MEGGITT, Mervyn J.
Walbiri society, Central Australia.
  University of Sydney, 1955. M.A. iii, 484pp., diags., maps.
Publication:
Desert people: a study of the Walbiri Aborigines of Central Australia.
  Sydney, Angus and Robertson, 1962. 348pp. illus.

MELENDRES, Patricia Mediran
Social criticism in the Australian novel: the Aboriginal theme.
  Australian National University, 1967. M.A. iii, 279pp.

METCALFE, Christopher Douglas
An examination of the acculturation, adjustment and assimilation of racial minority groups to the wider community in western-European-type societies, with particular reference to the part-Aboriginal minority at Narrogin, Western Australia.
  University of Western Australia, 1960. B.A. 63pp.

An examination of minority group acculturation, adjustment and assimilation, with particular reference to the young, unmarried, part-Aboriginal population employed in the Perth metropolitan area.
  University of Western Australia, 1961. B.A. (Hons.). v, 99pp. map.

Bardi verb morphology: a transformational analysis.
  Australian National University, 1972. Ph.D. xii, 287pp. figs., map, tbls.
Publication:
Bardi verb morphology (northwestern Australia). Canberra, Australian National University Press, 1975. viii, 215pp. map.

MEUMANN, Frank Olaf
An anthroposcopic and anthropometric study of the skeleton of a full-blood female Tasmanian Aborigine (Truganini).
  University of Tasmania, 1971. B.Med. Sc.(Hons.). figs., pls., transparencies.

MICHA, Franz Josef
Eingeborenenhandel in Zentralaustralien.

[Trading by Central Australian Aborigines.]
Rheinische Friedrich-Wilhelms Universität, Bonn, 1957.
Phil.Fak.Diss. 251pp. figs., maps, tbls.

MIDDLETON Hannah
The land rights and civil rights campaign of the Gurindji at Wattie
Creek (an Australian manifestation of the world-wide national
liberation movement).
  Humboldt Universität, Berlin, 1972, Ph.D. 172, 20pp. diags., tbls.
  Publication:
  'Forschungreise nach Australien', *Ethnographisch-Archäologische*
  Zeitschrift, 12, 1971.

MILICH, Corinne
Official attitudes to the South Australian Aborigines in the 1930s.
  University of Adelaide, 1967. B.A. 97pp. tbl.

MINCHEN, Pamela
Indigenisation of the church: a study of the Lutheran and Methodist
missions.
  University of Western Australia, 1968. B.A. (Hons.). vi, 146pp.
  maps, pls.

MISTRATE-HAARHUIS, Johannus Gerhardus Maria
Report of an inventarisation of the Australian artefacts from the
following museums:
Rijksmuseum voor Volkenkunde, Leiden,
Koninklijk Instituut voor de Tropen, Amsterdam,
Museum voor Land-en Volkenkunde, Rotterdam,
Museum voor onderwijs, The Hague,
Museum Justinus Van Nassau, Breda,
Museum of the Institute for Cultural and Social Anthropology,
Nijmegen.
  Katholieke Universiteit, Nijmegen, 1971. Doctorandus. various
  pagings.

MITCHELL, Brian John
Fringe-dwelling existential despair.
  University of Queensland, 1968. B.Soc.St. (Hons.). vi, 112, [10]
  pp. figs., tbls.

MITCHELL, Ian S.
The inter-relationship of culture and language with special reference to Australian Aboriginal material.
University of Western Australia, 1961. B.A. (Hons.). 44pp.

MONK, Janice Jones
Socio-economic characteristics of six Aboriginal communities in Australia: a comparative ecological study.
University of Illinois at Urbana-Champaign, 1972. Ph.D. iv, 397pp.

MOODIE, Peter M.
(Published works)
University of Sydney, 1975. M.D.
Aboriginal health. Canberra, Australian National University Press, 1973. 307pp.
with E. B. Pedersen, *The health of Australian Aborigines: an annoted bibliography.* Canberra, Australian Government Publishing Service, 1971. 248pp.

MOODY, Mary L. A.
Missionary policy, methods and attitudes to native social organization and belief, with special reference to northern Australia.
University of Sydney, 1953. M.A. qualifying essay. iii, 28, 4pp.

A descriptive statement of the phonemics and morphology of Anindilyaugwa, the language of Groote Eylandt, Northern Territory.
University of Sydney, 1954. M.A. 80pp.

MOORE, David *see* BARKER, Geoffrey *et al.*

MOORE, David R.
The tribes of Cape York: a reconstruction of their way of life and a consideration of its relevance to the archaeological problems of the area.
University of Sydney, 1965. Dip.Anthrop. 136pp. illus., maps.
Publication:
'Cape York Aborigines and the Islanders of the Western Torres Straits' in D. Walker (ed.), *Bridge and barrier: the natural and cultural history of Torres Strait.* Canberra, Australian National University Press, 1971, pp.327-43.

MORLEY, John
The types, distribution and formation of Australian totemism.
University of Sydney, 1936. M.A. v, 105pp. map.

MORPHY, Howard
A re-analysis of the toas of the Lake Eyre tribes of Central Australia: an
examination of their form and function.
University of London, 1972. M.Phil. v, 235pp. illus., maps.

MORRISON, John
A cultural, physiological and pathological study of the Western Desert
Aborigines of Australia.
Glasgow University, 1974. M.D. viii, 493pp. illus., maps, pls.

MORTLOCK, Eversley Ruth
The educational attainment of part-Aboriginal children in two Western
Australian schools.
University of Western Australia, 1965. B.A. vi, 51pp. pl., tbls.

MOUNTFORD, Charles P.
The rock art of Australia.
Cambridge University, 1959. Dip.Anthrop. 202pp. illus., maps.

The Pitjandjara: their land and beliefs.
University of Adelaide, 1962. M.A. 2 v. (89, [2]pp.; vol. 2 56 pls.),
figs.

MOYLE, Alice M.
The intervallic structure of Australian Aboriginal singing.
University of Sydney, 1957. M.A. 123, 30pp. map, 72 music
transcriptions, 55 interval charts.

North Australian music: taxonomic approach to the study of
Aboriginal song performance.
Monash University, 1974. Ph.D. 946pp. figs., handgraphs, maps,
melographs, music notations, pls., song texts.

MULDOON, Shane
Empirical explorations into the social creation of Aboriginal deviance:
a study of images, behavioural expectations and behaviour exhibited by
both functionaries and Aborigines.
University of New England, 1973. B.A. (Hons.). 177pp. tbls.

MULHOLLAND, Beverley
The influence of the Pallotine Training Centre, Rossmoyne, on the
assimilation of people of part Aboriginal descent into the total
Australian community.
Education Department of Western Australia, Higher Teacher's
Certificate thesis, 1972. 214pp. illus.

MUNDY, Peter A.
The Chundeelee community: a study of reaction to acculturation.
    University of Western Australia, 1967. B.A. 51pp. tbls.

MUNN, Nancy D.
Walbiri graphic art and sand drawing: a study in the iconography of a Central Australian culture.
    Australian National University, 1960. Ph.D. viii, 189pp. charts, illus.

MURPHY, Thomas Roy
Studies on the mandible of the Australian Aborigine.
    University of Adelaide, 1957. 204pp. diag., illus., map, tbls.
Publications:
'The chin region of the Australian Aboriginal mandible', *American Journal of Physical Anthropology*, 15, 1957, 517-37.
'Changes in mandibular form during post-natal growth', *Australian Dental Journal*, 2, 1957, 267-76.
'Mandibular adjustment to functional tooth attrition', *Australian Dental Journal*, 3, 1958, 171-9.

The human occlusal plane: an annotated study.
    University of Edinburgh, 1961. M.D.S. 179pp. diags., tbls.
Publications:
'A biometrical study of the helicoidal occlusal plane of the worn Australian dentition', *Archives of Oral Biology*, 9, 1964, 255-67.
'The relationship between attritional facets and the occlusal plane in Aboriginal Australians', *Archives of Oral Biology*, 9, 1964, 269-80.
'The progressive reduction of tooth cusps as it occurs in natural attrition', *Dental Practitioner*, 19, 1968, 8-14.

MURRAY-PRICE, Judith
Woman settlers and Aborigines.
    University of New England, 1973. B.A. (Hons.). ii, 127pp. maps.

MUTTON, Leslie A.
An examination of the economic features of the lives of Aborigines in the contact situation, with particular reference to those living in and near the city of Perth.
    University of Western Australia, 1965. B.A. v, 52pp. figs., map, tbls.

MYERS, Fred R.
What men do: a preliminary consideration of the classification of self in the universe of Aboriginal cultures.
    Bryn Mawr College, 1972. M.A. 146pp. maps.

NADEL, George H.
Adaptation and social culture in early colonial Australia.
Harvard University, 1965. Ph.D. 450pp.

NAILON, Daphne Catherine
Christian education in the Aboriginal culture: a survey of relevant literature.
Monash University, 1973. M.Ed. vii, 82pp. illus.

NELSON, Hyland Neil
Early attempts to civilise the Aborigines of the Port Phillip District.
University of Melbourne, 1966. M.Ed. 262, ix pp.
Publication:
'The missionaries and the Aborigines in the Port Phillip District',
Historical Studies, Australian and New Zealand, 12 (45), 1965, 57-67.

NETTLE, Edward Bruce
What do children know about Aborigines?
Macquarie University, 1975. M.A. xiii, 241pp. diags., illus., maps, pls, tbls.

NEUHAUS, John W. G.
Ethnological dating with radioactive carbon.
University of New South Wales, 1965. M.Sc. v, 99pp. figs., pls., tbls.

NICHOLLS, Edward Brooke
A contribution to the study of the teeth of the Australian and Tasmanian Aboriginals.
University of Melbourne, 1913. D.D.S. 48pp. tbls.

NICHOLSON, Alexander Alan
Criteria used by Aboriginal and white Australian children in the selection of an information source.
University of Queensland, 1972. B.A. (Hons.). iv, 25pp. figs., tbls.

NIXON, Pamela
The integration of the half-caste community of La Perouse, New South Wales.
University of Sydney, 1948. M.A. 207pp. diags., maps, tbls.

NOLAN, Janette G.
Pastor J. G. Haussmann, a Queensland pioneer, 1838-1901.
University of Queensland, 1964. B.A. (Hons.). 122pp.

NOON, John Alfred
The analysis and comparison of names applied to moieties present in
Australian tribes.
  University of Pennsylvania, 1936. M.A. 17pp. 2 folders, maps.

NORTHEY, Ronald W.
The influence of a mission environment on committed part-Aboriginal
children.
  Education Department of Western Australia, Teacher's Higher
  Certificate thesis, 1967. 111pp. illus.

OATES, Lynette Frances
A tentative description of the Gunwinggu language of western Arnhem
Land.
  University of Sydney, 1953. M.A. (Hons.). 120pp. tbls.
  Publication:
  *A tentative description of the Gunwinggu language (of western Arnhem
  Land).* Sydney, University of Sydney, 1964. 120pp. Oceania
  Linguistic Monograph No. 10.

O'GRADY, Geoffrey Noel
Significance of the circumcision boundary in Western Australia.
  University of Sydney, 1959. B.A. 187pp. maps, tbls.

────────
Nyanamata grammar
  Indiana University, 1963. Ph.D. 135pp.
  Publication:
  Nyanamata grammar. Sydney, University of Sydney, 1964. xv, 90pp.
  Oceania Linguistic Monograph No. 9.

O'KELLY, Gregory John
The Jesuit Mission stations in the Northern Territory, 1882-1899.
  Monash University, 1967. B.A. (Hons.). v, 119pp. pls., tbls.
  Publication:
  Australia's Catholic Church. Melbourne, Dove Community
  Publications, 1973. 46pp.

OLDMEADOW, Kenneth Scot
The science of man: scientific opinion on the Australian Aborigines in
the late nineteenth century — the impact of evolutionary theory and
racial myth.
  Australian National University, 1969. B.A. (Hons.). [7], 71,
  [19]pp.

OSBORNE, Charles Roland
A grammar of the Tiwi language of north Australia.
University of London, 1970. Ph.D. 243pp.

OSTAPCHUK, Vanentina
A study in culture change: the Aborigines of Yorke Peninsula and of Point Pearce Reserve.
University of Adelaide, 1969. B.A. (Hons.). ii, 277pp. diags., maps, plan, tbls.

OXER, Robin
Allawah Grove: an experiment in assimilation.
University of Western Australia, 1963. B.A. (Hons.). ix, 247pp. figs., maps.

PALMER, Claire W.
Education among primitive peoples.
Colorado State Teachers' College, 1933. M.A. 82pp.

PATCHING, Ronald A.
Native education in Western Australia: changes in offical policy since the report of 'The Special Committee on Native Matters' made on June 19th, 1958.
University of Western Australia, 1964. B.A. iii, 45pp.

PATERSON, Jennifer L.
Native administration and welfare in Western Australia.
University of Western Australia, 1957. B.A. (Hons.). 107, iii pp.

PATTERSON, Gordon A.
The native policy of Sir George Gipps.
University of Sydney, 1934, M.A. 181pp.

PEACOCK, Dennis P.
Point Pearce Aboriginal children in the classroom: social and academic progress.
University of Adelaide, 1971. B.A. (Hons.). viii, 142pp. figs., tbls.

PEAK, Grahame John
Achievement and orientation among part-Aborigines and European-Australians in New South Wales.
University of Sydney, 1966. M.A. qualifying essay. 79pp.

PEARCE, Robert Harwood
A discussion of the Australian backed blade tradition. Was it a cultural introduction or an independent innovation?
University of Western Australia, 1972. B.A. vi, 45pp. figs., tbls.
___
A selected annotated bibliography of some elements of Australian small tool stone industries.
University of Western Australia, 1974. M.A. (Preliminary). 322pp.

PEARSON, Michael
The Macintyre valley: field archaeology and ethno-history.
University of New England, 1973. B.A. (Hons.). vii, 113pp. maps, tbls.

PENTONY, Brian
The dream in Australian culture.
University of Western Australia, 1938. B.A. (Hons.). 90pp.

PETER, Hanns
Typisierung der höheren wesen in Glaubensbereich der Eingeborenen Nordaustraliens
[A typology of beliefs in supernatural beings of north Australian Aborigines.]
Universität Wien, 1964. Phil. Fak.Diss. 207pp.

PETERSEN, Lindy
The performance of Aboriginal children on verbal and non-verbal tests of intelligence.
Flinders University of South Australia, 1974. M.Psych. 35pp.

PETERSON, Nicholas C.
The structure of two Australian Aboriginal ecosystems.
University of Sydney, 1971. Ph.D. xv, 123pp. figs., maps, pls., tbls.

PHILP, Hugh Whitelaw Stuart
Prejudice towards the Australian Aborigine.
Harvard University, 1958. Ph.D. various pagings, figs., illus., tbls.

PIERCE, Russell George
The effects of aquatic foods on the diet and economy of the Aborigines of the north coast of New South Wales at the time of the first settlement.
University of New England, 1971. B.A. (Hons.). 83pp. figs., pls., maps.

PIERSON, James Culhane
Aboriginality in Adelaide: urban resources and adaptations.
University of Washington (St. Louis), 1972. Ph.D. xviii, 447pp.
diags., tbls.

PILLING, Arnold Remington
Law and feud in an Aboriginal society of north Australia.
University of California (Berkeley), 1958. Ph.D. vii, 377pp. maps,
pls.
Publication:
'A historical versus non-historical approach to social change and
continuity among the Tiwi', *Oceania*, 32, 1962, 321-6.

PINCHES, Michael D.
A socio-cultural approach to Aboriginal housing.
University of Melbourne, 1973. B.Arch. 194pp. diags., figs., pls.,
tbls.

PIPER, Adrian
Ocean beach to mountain top. The Tweed Valley, New South Wales, in
prehistory.
University of New England, 1976. B.Litt. vi, 203pp. figs., pls., tbls.

PLATT, John T.
An introductory grammar of the Gugada dialect.
Monash University, 1968. M.A. 176pp. tbls.
Publication:
An outline grammar of the Gugada dialect. Canberra, Australian
Institute of Aboriginal Studies, 1972. (Australian Aboriginal Studies
No. 48, Linguistic Series No. 20) 68pp. tbls.

PLUMMER, Orlay Edward
The Murngin controversy.
Florida State University, 1970. M.A. 102pp. figs., tbls.

PÖCH, Rudolf
Studien an Eingeborenen von Neu-Südwales und an australischen
Schädeln.
[Studies of Aborigines of N.S.W. and studies of Australian skulls.]
Ludwig-Maximilian-Universität, Munich, 1915. Phil.Fak.Diss.
94pp.

POHLNER, Bernard H.
A comparison of two different approaches to teaching English in
Pitjantjatjara Aboriginal schools.

Western Teachers' College, Adelaide, 1972. Advanced Diploma. vi, 107, xlvii, [7]pp. figs., pls., tbls.

POINER, Gretchen
The process of the year : towards a model of prehistoric economic life on the New South Wales central and south coast.
University of New South Wales, 1971. B.A. 174pp. figs., maps, tbls.

POPE, Kathleen
An examination of the material culture of south eastern Cape York Peninsula, based on the Roth Ethnological Collection at the Australian Museum, Sydney.
University of Sydney, 1967. Dip.Anthrop. iv, 168pp. diags., illus., maps.

POWELL, Georgina M.
A field study of six part-Aboriginal families in Perth.
University of Western Australia, 1965. B.A. iii, 50pp. fig., pls.

POWELL, Terence Michael
Socio-economic exchange in Aboriginal Australia.
University of Western Australia, 1971. B.A. viii, 74pp.

POWER, Shane *see* BUSBY, Frank *et al.*

PRENTIS, Malcolm David
Aborigines and Europeans in the Northern Rivers region of New South Wales, 1823-1881.
Macquarie University, 1972. M.A. (Hons.). ix, 362pp. illus., map.

PRIDEAUX, David J.
The education of Aboriginal children in Adelaide: a comparative study.
University of Adelaide, 1971. B.A. (Hons.). iv, 162pp. illus., tbls.

Education and race relations: the effect of a course on race relations in Australia on the racial attitudes of teacher education students.
University of New England, 1974. M.Ed. [2], 53pp. tbls.

QUINE, Susan
Achievement orientation of Aboriginal and white Australian adolescents.
Australian National University, 1973. Ph.D. xi, 393pp. tbls.

QUINLIVAN, Francis Murray
The impact of the European on the American Indian and the Australian Aborigine.
University of Western Australia, 1961, B.A. 27pp.

QUISENBERRY, Kay
Dance in Arnhem Land: a field study project 1970-1972.
Southern Methodist University, Texas, 1973. M. Fine Arts. 164pp. diags., pls.

RAHILL, Michael see BARKER, Geoffrey et al.

RALPH, Felicity
Problem of the present.
University of Western Australia, 1967. B.A. iii,46,6,iii pp. maps.

RAMMER, Josef
Untersuchungen über Sexualleben und Ethik der südaustralischen Eingeborenen.
[Examination of the sex life and ethics of the South Australian Aborigines.]
Universität Wien, 1938. Phil.Fak.Diss. 314pp.

RANDELL, Alan E.
Number concepts of grade one European and part-Aboriginal children in rural schools in Western Australia.
University of Western Australia, 1969. M.Ed. ix, 158pp. diags., tbls.

RANDOLPH, Peter John
Urban Aboriginal sub-culture; determining that urban dwellers of Aboriginal descent can be conceptualised as and exhibit the conforming behaviour of a sub-culture entity, with special reference to those living in the metropolitan area of Perth, Western Australia.
University of Western Australia, 1972. B.Sc. (Hons.). v, 78pp. tbls.

RANKIN, Donald Hamilton
The history of the development of education in Western Australia.
University of Western Australia, 1924. M.A. 320pp.

RAO, Pappu Durga Prasada
The anatomy of the distal limb segments of the Aboriginal skeleton.
University of Adelaide, 1966. M.Sc. 293pp. figs., pls., tbls.

Study of finger and palmar prints in some tribes of India and Australia.
Utkal University, Orissa, India, 1970. Ph.D. 94, xxiii pp. fig., tbls.

RAYNER, Keith
The attitudes and influence of the churches in Queensland in matters of
social and political importance (1859-1914).
University of Queensland, 1951. B.A. (Hons.). 203pp.
_____
The history of the Church of England in Queensland.
University of Queensland, 1962. Ph.D. 2 v. ([10], 656pp.)

REAY, Marie
Kinship amongst the mixed-blood Aborigines in New South Wales.
University of Sydney, 1947. M.A.
    No further details are known of this thesis. The Library of
    the University of Sydney has lost its copy and the author's personal
    copy was lost in a flood.

REDDY, Coral Ann
South Queensland Aboriginal English: a study of the informal
conversational speech habits of two Aboriginal communities in the area,
with special reference to four male speakers of the 9-12 age group in the
closed community of Cherbourg.
University of Queensland, 1961. B.A. (Hons.). xii, 317pp.

REECE, Robert H.
The Aborigines and colonial society in New South Wales before 1850,
with special reference to the period of the Gipps administration, 1836-
1846.
University of Queensland, 1969. M.A. 2 v. (xxiii, 291pp.). illus.,
maps.
Publication:
Aborigines and colonists: black and white in colonial society in New
South Wales in the 1830s and 1840s. Sydney, Sydney University
Press, 1974. 264pp. illus.

REES, Jennifer
Contact with the Aborigines in the Kimberleys from 1872-1914.
    Claremont Teachers' College, 1965. History thesis.
        Although this item is mentioned in the literature it has not been
        possible to locate a copy.

REID, Beverley J.
White Australian attitudes towards Aborigines.
Monash University, 1974. B.A. (Hons.). 81pp.

REID, Susan Carol
Rhythmic analysis of verses from the Ngiyari/Langka Cycle of
Indulkana, South Australia.
University of Adelaide, 1975. B.Mus. (Hons.). 6 pages of drawings, 1
attached diagram and a recorded tape.

REIM, Helmut
Die Insektennahrung der Australischen Ureinwohner: eine Studie zur
Frühgeschichte menschlicher Wirtschaft und Ernährung.
[Insects as food of the Australian Aborigines: a study of the early
history of human economy and nutrition.]
Karl-Marx-Universität, Leipzig, 1961. Phil.Fak.Diss. 158pp.
Publication:
Die Insektennahrung der Australischen Unreinwohner: eine Studie zur
Frühgeschichte Menschlicher Wirtschaft und Ernährung. Berlin,
Akademie-Verlag, 1962. 158pp.

RENNIE, Joan
Assmilation, accommodation and intervention in Aboriginal education.
University of New England, 1971. B.A. (Hons.). vii, 147pp. tbls.

REYNOLDS, Patricia Anne
The religious status of Australian Aboriginal women.
University of Western Australia, 1962. B.A. ii, 27pp.

REYNOLDS, Peter Alan
Totemism in Aboriginal Australia.
University of Western Australia, 1962. B.A. ii, 22pp.

———
The social and cultural factors influencing the formal educational
achievements of children of Aboriginal descent.
University of Western Australia, 1973. M.A. preliminary essay.
102pp.

RICHARDSON, Barry E.
Myth and reality: an exploration of the development of the Aboriginal
theme in the Australian novel.
University of New England, 1969. B.Litt. 244pp.

RICHTER, Brigitte
Kinderleben bei den Australischen Eingeborenen vornehmlich den
Kimberleystämmen.
[Life of the children of the Australian Aborigines especially of the
Kimberley tribes.]
Georg-August-Universität zu Göttingen, 1958. Phil.Fak.Diss. 276pp.

ROBBINS, Elizabeth Jane
Tribal society: settler society: a comparison of political relations in Australia, New Zealand and the United States.
University of Adelaide, 1976. B.A. (Hons.). 74pp.

ROBERTSON, Alexander Milne
Anthropological account of the Aborigines of Western Australia, together with the climate, the diseases and the productions of the country.
Edinburgh University, 1883. M.D. iii, 84pp.
Publication:
Report upon peculiar habits and customs of the Aborigines of Western Australia, to accompany the collection of weapons, implements, etc., to the exhibition at Sydney, N.S.W. Perth, Government Printer, 1879. 8pp.

ROBIN, Arthur de Quetteville
The life of Mathew Blagden Hale, with special reference to the Australian church and community.
University of Western Australia, 1971. Ph.D. iv, 383pp. map, pls., tbls.

ROBINSON, Michael V.
Barton's Hill: a social anthropological study of a medium security prison and Aboriginal prisoners.
University of Western Australia, 1967. B.A. (Hons.). 113pp. diag., pls., tbls.
Publication:
'Imprisonment of Aborigines and part-Aborigines in Western Australia' in R. M. Berndt (ed.), *Thinking about Australian Aboriginal welfare.* Perth, University of Western Australia Press, 1969, pp.14-19.

———
Change and adjustment among the Bardi of Sunday Island.
University of Western Australia, 1973. M.A. x, 354pp. diag., figs., maps, pls.

ROCHE, Alexander Francis
I. An investigation of axonmyelin relationships with special reference to peripheral neuromuscular mechanisms.
II. Age changes in the skeleton of the Australian Aborigine.
University of Melbourne, 1954. Ph.D. various pagings. illus., tbls.

ROGERS, Carole
A study of the integration of two groups of Aboriginal families in Brisbane.
  University of Queensland, 1965. B.Soc.St. iv, 66pp. figs., tbls.

ROGERS, Peter Hugh
The industrialists and the Aborigines: a study of Aboriginal employment in the mining industry.
  University of Melbourne, 1969. M.App.Sci. iii, [4], 263pp. diags, illus., maps, tbls.

ROSE, Frederick G. G.
Classification of kin, age structure and marriage amongst the Groote Eylandt Aborigines: a study in method and a theory of Australian kinship.
  Humboldt Universität, Berlin, 1958. Phil.Fak.Diss. 572pp.
Publication:
Classification of kin, age structure and marriage, amongst the Groote Eylandt Aborigines: a study in method and a theory of Australian kinship. Berlin, Akademie-Verlag, 1960. xvi, 572pp. (also *Völkerkundliche Forschungen* Bd 3).

ROSEWARNE, Stuart Charles
Aborigines in colonial Queensland: an analysis of the Aborigines' response to colonialization and the impact of this upon subsequent black-white relations.
  University of Melbourne, 1976. M.A. 267pp.

ROSIER, Veronica A.
Yamiwara: a social and musical analysis of a ceremony of the Aboriginal women of the Western Desert.
  Monash University, 1973. B.A. (Hons.). 175, [9]pp. figs., map, tbls., transcriptions.

ROY, Parimat Kumar
Part Aborigines of Moora: a study of socio-economic integration and assimilation in an Australian rural community.
  University of Western Australia, 1968. M.A. 330pp. maps, pls.
Publications:
'History of administration and policy of Aboriginal welfare in Western Australia', *Journal of Social Research,* 12 (1), 1969.
'Part-Aborigines of Moora: factors hindering assimilation and integration', *Oceania,* 39 (4), 1969, 275-80.
'Education attainment of part-Aborigines in Western Australia', *Indian Anthropologist,* 2 (2), 1973.

RUSSO, George Henry
Bishop Salvado's plan to civilize and Christianize Aborigines (1846-
1900).
University of Western Australia, 1972. M.A. 270pp. pls.

RYAN, D'Arcy James
Australian totemism: a re-examination of the problem, with special
reference to recent fieldwork.
Oxford University, 1952. B.Litt. 272pp. diags.

RYAN, Lyndall
The Aborigines in Tasmania, 1800-1974 and their problems with
Europeans.
Macquarie University, 1975. Ph.D. xiii, 446pp. illus., map, tbls.

SABINE, Nigel
An ethnohistory of the Clarence Valley.
University of New England, 1970. B.A. (Hons.). various pagings.
maps, pls., tbls.

SACKETT, Lee
The Wiluna mob: kinship and marriage in a changing cultural context.
University of Oregon, 1975. Ph.D. 2 v. (xix, 117pp.). diags., tbls.

SADLER, Brenda
Cereal domestication: explanations for its occurrence in Palestine and
its non-occurrence in western New South Wales.
University of Sydney, 1975. B.A. (Hons.). 66pp. figs., maps, tbls.

SALTER, Michael A.
Games and pastimes of the Australian Aboriginal.
University of Alberta, 1967. M.A. xiv, 203pp. figs., illus., tbls.
Publication:
Games and pastimes of the Australian Aborigines. Eugene, Oregon,
Microcard Publications, 1967.

SAMPSON, Alfred James
A history of Weslyan Methodism in Western Australia.
University of Western Australia, 1958. M.A. 281pp. figs., pls., tbls.

SAVARTON, Stanislaw and GEORGE, Kenneth R.
A study of the historic, economic and socio-cultural factors which
influence Aboriginal settlements at Wilcannia and Weilmoringle,
N.S.W.
University of Sydney, 1971. B.Arch. 5 v. unpaged. maps, plans, pls.

SAXBY, H. Maurice
The history of Australian children's fiction 1841-1941: with reference where applicable to the ways in which these books have met the needs and interests of children.
> University of Sydney, 1965, M.Ed. vii, 400pp. illus.
> *Publication:*
> *A history of Australian children's literature, 1841-1941.* Sydney, Wentworth Books, 1969. xii, 212pp.

SCHEBECK, Bernard
Les systèmes phonologiques des langues australiennes.
[The phonological systems of Australian languages.]
> Université de Paris, 1972. Thèse lettres. v, 1274pp.

SCHMEICHEN, Hans Joachim
The Hermannsburg Mission Society in Australia, 1866-1895: changing missionary attitudes and their effects on the Aboriginal inhabitants.
> University of Adelaide, 1971. B.A. iii, 104pp. maps.

SCHULZE, John Michael
Body-build and dentofacial associations in Australian Aborigines: a metric study of morphological characters.
> University of Adelaide, 1973. M.D.S. xiii, 193pp. figs., pls., tbls.

SCOTT, William Maxwell
The educational and social problems of the Moore River Settlement.
> Education Department of Western Australia, Teacher's Higher Certificate thesis, 1963. 62pp.

SEE, Richard E.
Comparison of some Australian languages.
> University of California (Los Angeles), 1965. Ph.D. 148pp.

SELLICK, Joanne
A stylistic survey of Aboriginal art, with special reference to possible contacts within Oceania.
> University of Western Australia, 1971. B.A.(Hons.). 64pp. maps, pls., tbls.

SHANNON, Cynthia
Walpiri women's music: a preliminary study.
> Monash University, 1971. B.A.(Hons.). 4, iv, 201pp. diags., maps, music.

SHAPIRO, Warren
Miwuyt marriage: social structural aspects of the bestowal of females in
northeast Arnhem Land.
   Australian National University, 1969. Ph.D. vii, 213pp. illus., maps,
   pls., tbls.

SHARP, Richard Lauriston
The social anthropology of a totemic system in North Queensland,
Australia.
   Harvard University, 1937. Ph.D. xiii, 355pp. pls., tbls.
Publications:
'An Australian Aboriginal population', *Human Biology*, 12, 1940, 481-
   507.
'Steel axes for stone age Australians' in E. H. Spicer (ed.), *Human
   problems in technological change*. New York, Russell Sage Foun-
   dation, 1952, pp.69-90.
'People without politics' in Verne F. Ray (ed.), *Systems of political
   control and bureaucracy in human societies. Proceedings.* American
   Ethnological Society, 1958, pp.1-8.
'Hunter social organization: some problems of method' in Richard B.
   Lee and I. DeVore (eds.), *Man the hunter*. Chicago, Aldine, 1968,
   pp.158-61.

SHARPE, Christine
Prehistoric art in Australia.
   Melbourne College of Education, 1972. Thesis, secondary art and
   craft fine arts course. [3], 62pp. pls.

SHAW, Bruce C.
Social relations and commitments in a planned new town in Western
Australia.
   University of Western Australia, 1975. Ph.D. xvi, 416pp. figs., tbls.

SHEEHAN, Desmond Allen
A history of legislation for natives in Western Australia.
   Education Department of Western Australia, Teacher's Higher
   Certificate thesis, 1965. 52pp.

SHELMERDINE, Stephen Ross
The Port Phillip Native Police Corps as an experiment in Aboriginal
policy and practice, October 1837-January 1853.
   University of Melbourne, 1972. B.A. (Hons.). 24, [30]pp.

SHEPHERD, Brian W.
A history of the pearling industry of the north-west coast of Australia from its origins until 1916.
University of Western Australia, 1976. M.A. 195pp.

SHERWOOD, John L.
The use of the vernacular in the education of the Australian Aborigines, with special reference to the policy of assimilation.
University of Western Australia, 1964. B.A. 34pp.

SIEBER, Albert David
The treatment of the sick in non-literate societies, with special reference to the traditional Aboriginal Australian society.
University of Western Australia, 1968. iii, 57pp. map.

SLARKE, Phyllis E.
An examination of inter-racial group relations of racial minority groups considered in the context of the wider social groups in Western European-type societies, with particular reference to the part-Aboriginal minority in Gnowangerup, Western Australia.
University of Western Australia, 1961. B.A.
References to this thesis have been noted but it has not been possible to locate a copy.

SLUGGETT, Rosalie J.
Change and non-change in an Aboriginal community, Warburton Ranges, Western Australia.
University of Adelaide, 1973. B.A. (Hons.). 111pp. figs., maps, pls., tbls.

SMALL, Michael William
Some aspects of education in Western Australia raised during the 23rd-26th Parliament (1959-1970).
University of Western Australia, 1971. M.Ed. 196pp. tbls.

SMITH, Bernard W.
A study of European art and related ideas in contact with the Pacific 1768-1850.
Australian National University, 1957. Ph.D. xvii, 527pp. 214 reproductions of paintings, water-colours, medallions, etc.
Publication:
European vision and the South Pacific 1788-1850: a study in the history of art and ideas. Oxford, Clarendon Press, 1960. xviii, 287pp. pls.

SMITH, Kenwyn Kingsford
A validation of the Queensland Test: a cross-cultural study of the cognitive capacity of a sample of European children from Taringa State School and a sample of Aboriginal children from Cherbourg State School.
University of Queensland, 1966. B.A. (Hons.). 81pp. diags., tbls.

SMITH, Leonard Robert
The Aboriginal population of Australia.
University of New South Wales, 1976. Ph.D. 385, xx pp. figs., tbls.

SMYTHE, Charles W.
Environment in the universe: totemic identity in central Australia, the comparison of two Australian societies.
University of Missouri, 1973. M.A. 112, [1]pp. map.

SNOOKS, Diane
Australian Aborigines: economical opportunities.
University of Western Australia, 1968. B.A. 39pp.

SOKOLOFF, Boris Alexander
The Worimi hunter-gatherers at Port Stephens: an ethnohistory.
University of New England, 1975. B.A. (Hons.). vii, 175pp. diags., pls., tbls.

SOMMER, Bruce Arthur
Kunjen phonology: sychronic and diachronic.
University of Hawaii, 1968. M.A. [6], 122, 5pp. maps, tbls.
Publication:
Kunjen phonology: synchronic and diachronic. Canberra, Australian National University, 1969. (Pacific Linguistics Series B — Monograph No. 11) 72pp. maps, tbls., bibliog.

Kunjen syntax: a generative view.
University of Hawaii, 1970. Ph.D. xii, 363pp. diags., tbls.
Publication:
Kunjen syntax: a generative view. Canberra, Australian Institute of Aboriginal Studies, 1972. (Australian Aboriginal Studies No. 45, Linguistic Series No. 19) 160pp. tbls., figs., bibliog.

SOMERLAD, Elizabeth A.
The importance of ethnic identification for assimilation and integration: a study of Australian Aborigines' attitudes.
University of Sydney, 1968. B.A. (Hons.). various pagings. diags., tbls.

Publications:
with J. W. Berry, 'The role of ethnic identification in distinguishing between attitudes towards assimilation and integration of a minority racial group', *Human Relations*, 23, 1970, 23-9.
Reprinted in G. Kearney, P. R. de Lacey and G. R. Davidson (eds.), *The psychology of Aboriginal Australians.* Sydney, Wiley, 1973, pp.236-43.

The impact of formal education on the personal identity of Australian Aboriginal adolescents.
Australian National University, 1972. Ph.D. xxii, 298pp. figs., map, tbls.

SOUTH, Terry R.
Giyum: a review of Queensland Aboriginal linguistics, 1770-1963.
University of Queensland, 1972. B.A. (Hons.). iii, 143pp. map, tbls.

STANNER, William Edward Hanley
Culture contact on the Daly river.
University of Sydney, 1932. Draft of M.A. thesis. various pagings.
Held at Australian Institute of Aboriginal Studies, Canberra.

Economic changes in north Australian tribes.
University of London, 1938. Ph.D. various pagings.

STANTON, John E.
Coomealla; at the merging of the waters: a study of ethnic interaction in a bi-cultural community on the New South Wales-Victorian border of Australia.
University of Auckland, 1972. M.A. [7], 99, xlviii pp. maps, tbls.

STEVENS, Francis Seymour
Industrial and race relations in northern Australia.
University of New South Wales, 1973. Ph.D. 2 v. (xii, 646, 41pp.). tbls.

STEWART, Shelley Jane
An investigation of visual imagery function in Aboriginal children at varying levels of assimilation.
University of New England, 1972, B.A. (Hons.). i, 125pp.
Publication:
with P. W. Sheehan, 'A cross-cultural study of eidetic imagery among Australian Aboriginal children', *Journal of Social Psychology*, 87, August 1972, 179-88.

STOCKBRIDGE, Margaret.Elizabeth
Female teenage delinquents in Western Australia.
University of Western Australia, 1974. Ph.D. 700pp. figs., tbls.

STOCKTON, James Harold
Report of an archaeological survey in the vicinity of Bribie Island,
south-east Queensland.
University of Queensland, 1973. B.A. 140pp.

STONE, Sharman
The experience of the Australian Aborigine in white Australia, 1788-
1972.
Monash University, 1972. B.A. [50]pp. fig., illus.

STORER, Desmond S.
The social power structure and decision-making processes in a West
Australian country town: with regard to recent changes in such
structure and processes due to the recent introduction of a large
aluminium refinery.
University of Western Australia, 1973. M.A. xviii, 431pp. figs.,
maps, pls., tbls.

STREHLOW, Theodor George Henry
An Aranda grammar.
University of Adelaide, 1938. M.A. iii, 108pp.

STRUWE, Ruth
Forschungsgeschichte und Forschungstand der Archäologie zur
urspunglichen Besiedlung Australiens.
[History and state of research into archaeology of the early civilisation
of Australia.]
Humboldt Universität, Berlin, 1968. Diplomabeit angefertigt. 44pp.

_____

Untersuchungen zum älteren Abschnitt der Urgeschichte Australiens
aufgrund einer Analyse der Steinindustrien Australiens und dreier
Fundkomplexe aus Neuguinea und Indonesien.
[Research into the prehistory of Australia based upon the examination
of stone implement quarries and three assemblages from New Guinea
and Indonesia.]
Humboldt Universität, Berlin, 1974. Phil.Fak.Diss. 2 v. (275pp.).
diags., illus., maps, pl, tbls.

STURKEY, Robert Douglas
The growth of the pastoral industry in the north west, 1862-1901.
University of Western Australia, 1957. B.A.(Hons.). various
pagings. tbls.

SULLIVAN, Katherine M.
The archaeology of Mangat and some of the problems of analysing a
quartz industry.
University of Sydney, 1973. B.A. (Hons.). various pagings. figs.,
illus., maps, pls., tbls.

SULLIVAN, Sharon M.
The material culture of the Aborigines of the Richmond and Tweed
Rivers of northern New South Wales at the time of the first white
settlement.
University of New England, 1964. B.A.(Hons.). xii, 192, [6]pp.
illus., maps.

The traditional culture of the Aborigines of north western New South
Wales.
University of New England, 1970. M.A. iv, [2], 303pp. illus., maps,
tbls.

SURMON, Albert Vale
A survey of non-governmental organizations in Sydney concerned with
Aboriginal affairs.
University of Sydney, 1964. B.A. (Hons.), [4], 106, 4pp. figs.

SUTTON, Peter John
Gugu-Badhun and its neighbours: a linguistic salvage study.
Macquarie University, 1973. M.A. (Hons.). 272pp. maps.

SWAN, Barbara M.
A method of analysis applied to coastal midden surface collections from
northern New South Wales.
University of Sydney, 1970. B.A. [5], 147pp. figs., illus., maps, tbls.

TAAL, Badara Saja
The respect factor in racial politics: a comparative study of race
relations in Australia, South Africa and New Zealand.
University of New England, 1976. M.A.(Hons.). 455pp.

TANG, You Liang
Essai sur les movements de la population dans l'océan Pacifique.

[A study of population movements in the Pacific Ocean region.]
Université de Toulouse, 1934. Thèse doctorat en droit. 355pp.

TARAGEL, Anna Joyce
Assertion of identity and nativism as strategies for relieving the marginal situation of Aborigines in the Australian society.
University of Sydney, 1972. B.A. iii, 74pp. map.

TATZ, Colin Martin
Aboriginal administration in the Northern Territory of Australia.
Australian National University, 1964. Ph.D. [8], xii, 423pp. tbls.
Accompanied by a volume of enclosures, illus., and facsimiles.

TAYLOR, Daryl J.
The challenge of the outback in Australian education 1900 to 1940.
University of Sydney, 1969. M.Ed. 197pp. maps, tbls.

TAYLOR, John C.
Race relations in south-east Queensland, 1840-1860.
University of Queensland, 1967. B.A. (Hons.). ii, 184pp. maps.

TAYLOR, Narelle
The native mounted police of Queensland, 1850-1900.
University of Queensland, 1970. B.A. (Hons.). 94pp. tbls.

TEASDALE, George Robert
Psycholinguistic abilities and early experience: a study of children from different ethnic and socio-economic backgrounds.
University of New England, 1972. Ph.D. xiv. 359pp. tbls.
Publications:
with F. M. Katz, 'Psycholinguistic abilities of children from different ethnic and socio-economic backgrounds', *Australian Journal of Psychology*, 20, 1968, 155-9.
'Validity of the PPVT as a test of language ability with lower SES children', *Psychological Reports*, 25, 1969, 746.
'Language disabilities of children from lower socio-economic and part-Aboriginal backgrounds', *Australian Journal of Mental Retardation*, 2, 1972, 69-74.
'Psycholinguistic abilities and maternal language style: a study of young children from disadvantaged backgrounds'. Paper read to the *Fifth International Seminar on Special Education*, Melbourne, 20-24 August 1972.

TEASDALE, Jennifer Irene
Aboriginal matrifocality: a situational analysis.
University of New England, 1971. M.Ec. viii, 282pp.

TER WEER, Martinus Clara
Altruisme bij enkele natuurvolken van Afrika en Australia.
[Altruism among the indigenous peoples of Africa and Australia.]
University of Amsterdam, 1939. Ph.D. 124, [3]pp.

TERWIEL-POWELL, Fiona Jane
Developments in the kinship system of the Hope Vale Aborigines: an analysis of changes in the kinship nomenclature and social structure of the KuKu-Yimityirr Aborigines.
University of Queensland, 1976. Ph.D. 426pp.

TESTART, Alain
Des classifications dualistes en Australia.
[Dual classification in Australia.]
    Université de Paris, 1975. Thèse de troisième cycle. 251pp. diags., tbls.

TETLEY, George T.
A gallery for Aboriginal man.
    School of Architecture, South Australian Institute of Technology, 1966. Architecture thesis. iv, [7], 199, vii pp. pls., 21 sketch plans and detailed drawings.

THOMPSON, E. Winifred
The training of native children under six years.
    University of Western Australia. 1945. M.A. iv, 198pp. illus.

THOMPSON, Patricia Jill
A community approach to guided change among Australian Aborigines.
    University of Queensland, 1968. B.Soc.St. (Hons.). vii, 106pp. figs.

THOMSON, Donald Ferguson
Eight papers, including — the hero cult; initiation and totemism in north Queensland; notes on a hero cult from the Gulf of Carpentaria.
    University of Melbourne, 1934. D.Sc. various pagings.

Part I. Kinship and behaviour in north Queensland.
Part II. Names and naming in the Wik Monkan tribe.
    Cambridge University, 1951. Ph.D. 3 v. (123, 47pp.). 7 maps. In addition 15 separately published items were submitted.

Publication:
Kinship and behaviour in north Queensland: a preliminary account of
kinship and social organisation on Cape York Peninsula. Canberra,
Australian Institute of Aboriginal Studies, 1972. viii, 59pp. figs.,
map, pls.

THORNE, Alan Gordon
Craniometric study of modern racial groups and fossil crania, using new
instrumental and analytical techniques.
University of Sydney, 1964. M.A. qualifying essay. 32, iii, 111pp.
figs., pls., tbls.

The racial affinities of the Tasmanian Aborigines: some skeletal
evidence.
University of Sydney, 1967. M.A.(Hons.). 113pp. diags., pls., tbls.

Kow swamp and Lake Mungo; towards an osteology of early man in
Australia.
University of Sydney, 1975. Ph.D. 2 v. (x, 286; A1-115 pp.). figs.,
pls. Includes published papers in pocket.

TILBROOK, Lois J.
Socio-cultural adaptation of a sample of part-Aboriginal girls: Perth
Working Girls' Hostel residents.
University of Western Australia, 1973. M.A. xxiii, 452pp. figs.,
maps, tbls.

TILBY, Jenis Marie
Public opinion in Australia on South Africa's racial policies, 1959-61.
University of Adelaide, 1963. B.A.(Hons.). viii, 169pp. tbls.

TOMLINSON, John Richard
Community development with the South Brisbane Aboriginal
community
University of Queensland, 1974. M.Soc.Work. xi, 363pp. figs., tbls.

TONKINSON, John R.
Australian Aboriginal art: the Aranda and their tjurunga.
University of Western Australia, 1964. B.A. 35pp.

TONKINSON, Robert
Factors affecting movement and assimilation among part-Aborigines in
the Narrogin district.
University of Western Australia, 1962. B.A.(Hons.). xii, 155pp.
genealogies, maps, pls.

Social structure and acculturation of Aborigines in the Western Desert.
University of Western Australia, 1966. M.A. xvi, 358p. maps, pls.,
tbls.

Na:wajil: a Western Desert Aboriginal rainmaking ritual.
University of British Columbia, 1972. Ph.D. xxii, 319pp. tbls.

TOWNLEY, Patricia
An analysis of scrapers from Capertree.
University of Sydney, 1974. B.A. (Hons.). 56pp. figs., illus., map,
tbls.

TRAINOR, Doreen E.
The stigma of the fringe-dweller.
University of Western Australia, 1968. B.A. i, 29pp.

TREFRY, David
The theory of segmental phonology and its application to Dieri.
Macquarie University, 1974. Ph.D. ix, 443pp. diags., illus., tbls.

TRIEBELS, Leo Felix
Enige aspecten van de regenboogslang. Een vergelijkende studie.
[Some aspects of the Rainbow serpent. A comparative study.]
Katholieke Universiteit, Nijmegen, 1958. Ph.D. 142pp.

TRUDINGER, Ronald M.
Early attempts to educate Aborigines in eastern Australia from 1788 to
1888.
University of Sydney, 1973. M.A. vii, 236pp. illus.

TSUNODA, Tasaku
A grammar of the Warungu language, north Queensland.
Monash University, 1974. M.A. 662pp.

TULLY, Ann Clare
Totemism in Aboriginal Australia: a critical evaluation.
University of Western Australia, 1968. B.A. iii, 43pp. map.

TULLY, Maxwell Leslie
The educational use of Aboriginal myths and legends as an aid to
mutual understanding and assimilation.
Education Department of Western Australia, Teacher's Higher
Certificate thesis, 1969. 65pp.

TULSI, Ram Singh
The vertebral column of the Australian Aborigine: a morphological, metrical and radiographic study.
University of Adelaide, 1967. M.Sc. xviii, 247pp. illus., maps, pls., tbls.

TURNER, Daniel H.
The Wanungamagaljuagba and their neighbours: a study in adaptation.
University of Western Australia, 1971. Ph.D. [19], iii, 422pp. maps, pls.

TWYMAN, James E.
Genital operations among the Australian Aborigines.
Northwestern University, 1960. M.A. 228pp. figs., maps.

VALLANCE, Glen Alexander
The unwelcome hosts: part-Aborigines in a north-western New South Wales town.
University of Sydney, 1971. M.A. vi, 122pp. diags., pls., tbls.

VAN GEFFEN, Rumoldus Johannes Henricus M.
Geschiedenis en betekenis van het missiewerk onder de Aborigines van Australia.
[The history and significance of mission work among the Australian Aborigines.]
Katholieke Universiteit, Nijmegen, 1974. Doctoraal scriptie (approximately equivalent to M.A.). 111pp.

VAN GENT, Jacobus Josephus Maria
Geneeskunde en cultuur.
[Medicine and culture.]
Katholieke Universiteit, Nijmegen, 1967. Candidaats scriptie (approximately equivalent to B.A.). 41pp.

De Australische Aborigines.
[Australian Aborigines.]
Katholieke Universiteit, Nijmegen, 1969. Doctoraal scriptie (approximately equivalent to M.A.). 60pp.

VATTER, Ernst
Der australische Totemismus.
[Totemism in Australia.]
Universität Hamburg, 1925. Phil.Fak.Diss. 157pp.

VILLIERS, Linda E.
Magic and sorcery among the desert people and Arnhem Landers.
Monash University, 1973. B.A. (Hons.). 87pp. tbls.

VISSER, Cornelius F.
Über den Ursprung der Vorstellungen von tierischen Menschenahen bei den Eingeborenen Zentralaustraliens.
[About the origin of the conception of animal-like ancestors of the Aborigines of Central Australia.]
Karl-Marx-Universität, Leipzig, 1913. Phil.Fak.Diss. 122pp.
Publication:
Über den Ursprung der Vorstellungen von tierischen Menschenahen bei den Eingeborenen Zentralaustraliens. Weida, Thomas and Hubert, 1913. 122pp

VÖLGER, Gisela
Die Tasmanier, Versuch einer ethnographische-historischen Rekonstruktion.
[The Tasmanian: an ethno-historical reconstruction.]
Johannes Gutenberg-Universität, Mainz, 1972. Phil.Fak.Diss. 381pp. illus., maps, tbls.

VON GUHR, Gunter
Heirat und Verwandtschaftssystem bei den Aranda in Zentralaustralien (Kritik des sogenannten Aranda-Typs von Radcliffe-Brown).
[The marriage and kinship system of the Aranda in Central Australia (critique of the so-called Aranda type by Radcliffe-Brown).]
Humboldt Universität, Berlin, 1960. Phil.Fak.Diss. 217pp.

VON STURMER, Diane
Past masters now: a study of the relationship between anthropology and Australian Aboriginal societies.
University of Queensland, 1976. B.A. (Hons.). 230pp.

VON TIMM, Klaus
Die Bedeutung von Blut and rotem Ocker in der Vorstellungswelt der Australier.
[The meaning of blood and red ochre in the realm of imagination of the Australian Aborigine.]
Friedrich-Schiller Universität, Jena, 1962. Phil.Fak.Diss. 265pp.

WADDINGTON, Gwenda R.
An examination of factors which may contribute to the special degree of difficulty experienced by Aboriginal children in formal learning situations.
University of Sydney, 1974. M.Ed. 3 v. (xxiv, 334pp.). illus., tbls.

WAIT, Esther
Migration of people of Aboriginal ancestry to the metropolitan areas and their assimilation.
   University of Sydney, 1950. B.A. (Hons.). 156pp.

WALSH, Phillipa Barbara
The problem of native policy in South Australia in the nineteenth century, with particular reference to the Church of England Boindie Mission, 1850-1896.
   University of Adelaide, 1966. B.A. (Hons.). [3], viii, 164pp.

WALSTER, Robert John
Aboriginal children at school — a story of failure: an examination of the mal-performance of Aboriginal children in Australian schools.
   University of Western Australia, 1971. B.A. vi, 55pp.

WANNINGER, Josef
Das Heilige in der Religion der Australier: eine Untersuchung über den Begriff 'Tjurunga' bei den Aranda.
[The sacredness of the religion of the Australian Aborigine: an examination of the meaning of 'Tjuranga' with the Aranda.]
   Ludwig-Maximillians-Universität, Munich, 1926. Phil.Fak.Diss. viii, 137pp.
Publications:
'Das Heilige in der Religion der Australier', *Abbandlungen zur Philosphie und Psychologie der Religion Wissenschaft*, 1927,14-15.
Das Heilige in der Religion der Australier: eine Untersuchung über den Begriff 'Tjurunga' bei den Aranda. Würzburg, Becker, 1927. xviii, 137pp.

WARHURST, Christopher
The fantasy that they would disappear: the assimilation policy, the Federal Liberal government and their response to the May 1967 referendum. The administration of Aboriginal affairs, 1961-1973.
   Flinders University of South Australia, 1976. B.A. (Hons.). 87pp. figs., this

WATERS, Kenneth Newton
The education and assimilation of the Australian Aborigines, with special reference to those in Western Australia.
   Education Department of Western Australia, Teacher's Higher Certificate thesis, 1962. 155pp.

WATSON, Peter
A history of New Norcia.
   Education Department of Western Australia, Teacher's Higher Certificate thesis, 1968. 58pp.

WATTS, Betty H.
Some determinants of the academic progress of Australian Aboriginal adolescent girls.
University of Queensland, 1970. Ph.D. 2 v. (xxiii, 650pp.). figs., tbls.
Publications:
'Achievement-related values in two Australian ethnic groups' in W. J. Campbell (ed.), *Scholars in context: the effects of environments on learning.* Sydney, Wiley, 1970, pp.110-30.
'Personality factors in the academic success of adolescent girls' in G. E. Kearney, P. R. de Lacey and G. R. Davidson (eds.), *The psychology of Aboriginal Australians.* Sydney, Wiley, 1973, pp.277-87.

WEIGL, Maria
Zur australischen Kunst.
[Australian art.]
Universität Wien, 1936. Phil.Fak.Diss. 137pp.

WELBORN, Susan
Parliamentary attitudes to Aborigines in Queensland and Western Australia, 1897-1907.
University of Western Australia, 1975. B.A. (Hons.). 66pp.

WEST, Alan Lindsay
Adjustment of part-Aborigines trained on a rural south-west mission.
University of Western Australia, 1959. B.A. various pagings.

WEST, Anne H.
The education of native children in Western Australia.
University of Western Australia, 1953. B.Ed. 62pp.

WEST, Margaret K. C.
A classification of the stylistic characteristics of the rock art of south-east Cape York.
University of Queensland, 1976. B.A. (Hons.). 180pp., illus.

WHITE, Carmel
Plateau and plain: prehistoric investigations in Arnhem Land, Northern Territory.
Australian National University, 1967. Ph.D. viii, 510pp. diags., illus., maps, tbls.

WHITE, Neville Graeme
A study of genetic variation among four Arnhem Land Aboriginal
tribes.
  La Trobe University, 1972. B.Sc (Hons.). 128pp. figs., pls., tbls.

WHITWORTH, Alexander Edward Stephen
Bureaucracy as a maladaptive response to the onset of turbulence: the
case of Aboriginal affairs.
  University of Melbourne, 1975. B.A. (Hons.). 50, [7]pp. diag.

WILD, Stephen Aubrey
Walbiri music and dance in the social and cultural nexus.
  Indiana University, 1975. Ph.D. vi, 157pp. diags., map.

WILLIAMS, Donald
A study of children's roles in a rapidly changing Aboriginal community.
  University of Queensland, 1971. Ph.D. xviii, 456pp. figs., illus., tbls.
Publications:
'Innovation and research in Australian education: a study of children's
  roles in a rapidly changing Aboriginal community', *Australian
  Journal of Education*, 15, 1971, 338-9.
'At home, at school, at play: a study of Aboriginal children in Arnhem
  Land', *Special Schools Bulletin*, 9 (1), 1972, 2-5; 9 (2), 1972, 2-4;
  9 (3), 1972, 2-7.

WILLIAMS, Nancy Margaret
Northern Territory Aborigines under Australian law.
  University of California (Berkeley), 1973. Ph.D. [2], xxi, 292pp.
  maps, tbls.

WILLMINGTON, Susan Margaret
The Aborigine Protection Society.
  Saint David's University College, University of Wales, 1979. Ph.D. vi,
  309pp.

WILMOTT, Judy
The pearling industry in Western Australia, 1857-1913: a study in
isolation.
  University of Western Australia, 1975. B.A. (Hons.). 57pp.

WILPERT, Clara Barbara
Kosmogonische Mythen der Australischen Eingeborenen: das Konzept
der Schöpfung und Anthropogenese.

[Australian Aboriginal myths about the cosmos: the concepts of creation and the origin of man.]
Universität zu Köln, 1970. Phil.Fak.Diss. 380pp.

WILSON, Edward
The integration of the Aboriginal child into the communities of the Great Southern District of Western Australia.
Education Department of Western Australia, Teacher's Higher Certificate thesis, 1964. 87pp.

WILSON, John
Cooraradale: a study of changes in administrative structures in relation to a part-Aboriginal settlement population; the effects of administrative action on aspects of social organization of this population; and the social interaction patterns of the settlement residents with members of the wider community.
University of Western Australia, 1958. B.A. (Hons.). 4 v. (various pagings).

Authority and leadership in a 'new style' Aboriginal community: Pindan, Western Australia.
University of Western Australia, 1961. M.A. xii, 418pp. diags., maps, pls.

WILSON, Katrin
The allocation of sex roles in social and economic affairs in a 'new style' Australian Aboriginal community: Pindan, Western Australia.
University of Western Australia, 1961. M.Sc. xii, 228pp. illus., maps., tbls.

WOLKENBERG, Linda
An evaluation of the concept of marginality as applied to the part-Aborigines of south-eastern Australia.
Monash University, 1970. B.A. (Hons.). 80pp. map.

WORSLEY, Peter Maurice
The changing social structure of the Wanindiljaugwa.
Australian National University, 1954. Ph.D. xviii, 394pp.

WUNDERLY, James
The cranial and other skeletal remains of Tasmanians in collections in the Commonwealth of Australia.
University of Melbourne, 1939. D.Sc. 35pp. pls., tbls.

Publication:
'The cranial and other skeletal remains: collections in the Commonwealth of Australia', *Biometrika*, 30, Pts. III and IV; 30 January 1939, 305-40. pls., tbls.

WUNDERSITZ, Joyleen P.
A reconstruction of the cultural history of the lower Murray River.
University of Adelaide, 1971. B.A. (Hons.). v, 129pp. illus., maps, tbls.

WYLLIE, Mabel G.
A study of polygymous marriage, with special reference to north Australia and Papua-New Guinea and the attitude thereto of the administration and the Christian missions.
University of Sydney, 1951. M.A. [2], 4, 180pp. tbls.

YALDEN, Peter
The Bondaian culture in eastern New South Wales: a study in prehistoric assemblage variation.
University of New England, 1974. B.A. (Hons.). vi, 196pp. figs., pls., tbls.

YALLOP, Colin L.
A description of the Aljawara language.
Macquarie University, 1970. Ph.D. 342pp.

YOUNG, Cully C.
Native education: a survey of the problems of natives in the Salmon Gums District.
Education Department of Western Australia, Teacher's Higher Certificate thesis, 1962. 95pp.

SUBJECT INDEX

A

ABORIGINES — BIBLIOGRAPHY
Gray, J. C.; Kershaw; Reynolds, Peter (1973)

ABORIGINES — MUSEUM COLLECTIONS
Mistrate-Haarhuis; Tetley

ADELAIDE, ABORIGINES IN
Edwards, D.; Forby; Gale; Hunt; Kewal; Killington; Knapman; Pierson; Prideaux (1971); Randolph

ABORIGINES' FRIENDS ASSOCIATION
Jenkins

ADELAIDE PLAINS
Ellis, R. W.

ALAWA LANGUAGE
Cunningham

ALCOHOL
Bain; Beckett (1958); Campbell, I. C.; Dufall; Hall, J. R.; Hart, P. R.; Lemaire; Lickiss

ALICE SPRINGS, ABORIGINES OF
Hartwig (1965); Harvey, A.

ALJAWARA LANGUAGE
Denham; Yallop

ALLAWAH GROVE
Dalton (1959); Oxer

ANINDILYAUGA LANGUAGE
Moody

ANTHROPOLOGY — BIBLIOGRAPHY
Gray, J. C.; Greenway; Moodie; Pearce (1974); Reynolds, Peter (1973)

ANTHROPOLOGY — GENERAL
Campbell, T. D.; Chase; Kommers; Krueger-Kelmar; Oldmeadow; Von Sturmer

ANTHROPOMETRY see Human Biology — Anthropometry, etc.

ARABANA TRADITIONS
Hercus

ARANDA LANGUAGE
Strehlow

ARANDA TRIBE
Boyall; Brown, M. W.; Campbell, T. D.; Crisp; Ellis, C. J.; Fine; Grandowski; Hackett; Hiatt, L. R. (1957); Knowles; Meagher (1960); O'Grady (1959); Schmeichen; See; Strehlow; Tonkinson, J. R.; Von Guhr; Wanninger

ARCHAEOLOGY — GENERAL
Allen, H. R. (1972); Bailey; Barbetti; Brayshaw; Coutts; Flood, J. M.
(1973); Hawke; Hope, G. S.; Jones, R.; Lourandos; McBryde; Macintosh;
Macknight; Meehan, B. F.; Moore, David R.; Pearson; Poiner; Sharpe;
Struwe (1968)

ARCHAEOLOGY — CAMP SITES, KITCHEN MIDDENS, CAVE
DEPOSITS, EXCAVATIONS
Allen, F. J.; Bailey; Barbetti; Bowdler; Campbell, V. M.; Coleman;
Collier; Coutts; Crawford (1969); Emerson; Flood, J. M.; Haglund-Calley;
Hume; Jones, R.; Lournados; McBryde; Meehan, B. F. (1976); Neuhaus;
Stockton; Swan; Sullivan, K. M., White, C.; Wundersitz; Yalden

ARNHEM LAND
Bern; Calley (1952); Glass; Hamilton; Hargrave; Harris, J. K.; Hiatt,
L. R.; Jones, T. A. (1953, 1958); Lawn; Layton; Macknight; Oates;
Plummer; Quisenberry; Sellick; Shapiro; Villiers; White, C.; White, N. G.;
Williams, D.; Williams, N. M.

ART *see* Visual Arts and Crafts

ARTEFACTS *see* Implements and Quarries

ASSIMILATION *see also* Urbanization
Bakker; Beatty; Beauchamp; Beckett; Bell, J. H.; Biddle; Burrage; Calley
(1959); Campbell, R.; Christophers; Clark; Dalton; De Lawyer; Dix;
Dryburgh; Edwards, D.; Farmer, R. L.; Fink (1955); Fitzpatrick; Flood,
J. B.; Gale; Harrison, C. M. A.; Hart, A. M.; Harvey, A.; Harvey, S. W.;
Herbert; Iredale; Johansons; Kilkelly; Kitson; Larsen; Le Sueur; McKeich
(1961); McMath; Metcalfe (1960); Milich; Mulholland; Nixon; Oxer;
Powell, G. M.; Ralph; Roy; Shaw; Sherwood; Sommerlad (1968); Stanton;
Tatz; Tilbrook; Tonkinson, R. (1962); Tully; Warhurst; West, A. H.;
Willmington; Wilson, E.

ATHERTON-EVELYN DISTRICT
Birtles

AYERS ROCK
Mountford (1962)

B

BAMYILI
Davidson, G. R. (1976)

BANDJALANG TRIBE
Calley (1955, 1959)

BARDI LANGUAGE
Metcalfe (1972)

BARDI TRIBE
Gibson; Metcalfe (1972); Robinson (1973)

BARTON'S HILL
Robinson (1967)

C

CAMP SITES *see* Archaeology — Camp Sites, etc.

CANNING RIVER
Green

CAPE YORK
Evans, K. E.; Hall, A. H. (1968); Moore; Pope; West, M. K. C.

CAVE DEPOSITS *see* Archaeology — Camp Sites, etc.

CEMETERY POINT
Collier

CENTRAL AUSTRALIA
Kirke; Lemaire; Micha; Morphy; Munn; Visser

CHANGE, CULTURAL AND CONSERVATISM
Adams; Armstrong, G.; Bell, D. R.; Blundell; Crawford (1969); Deakin; Dryburgh; Fink (1960); Grant; Graves; Green; Fitzgerald; Hausfeld (1972); Howell; Makin; Meggitt; Nadel; Powell, T. M.; Ralph; Robinson (1973); Rosier; Slugget; Stanner (1938); Tonkinson, R. (1966); Turner; Williams, D.; Wilson, J.; Wilson, K.

CHARLEVILLE,
Breen, R. M. (1976)

CHERBOURG
Guthrie

CHILDREN *see* Life Cycle — General

CHINNINGUM TRIBE
Martyn

CHRISTIANITY — INDIGENIZATION
Calley (1955, 1959); Minchen; Nailon; Taragel

CHUNDEELEE
Mundy

CHURCH OF ENGLAND
Rayner (1962)

CLARENCE VALLEY
Sabine

COLLIE
Harrison, C. M. A.

COMMUNITY WELFARE
Bakker; Bicknell; Chia; Giles; Halliwell; Hausfeld (1972); Henwood; Hickey; Knapman; Lovejoy; McDonnell; Mitchell, B. J.; Shaw; Thompson, P. J.; Tomlinson

CONCEPTION BELIEFS *see* Life Cycle — General, etc.

CONISTON
Hartwig (1960)

COOKING *see* Food — Types, etc.

COOMEALLA
Stanton
COORARADALE
Wilson, J. (1958)
CULTURAL DIFFUSION
Davidson, D. S. (1928) ; Davidson, G. R. (1976) ; Fraser; Kabo; Knowles; McCarthy; Mountford (1959) ; Moyle; O'Grady (1959) ; Pearce; Sellick; Twyman
CULTURAL CONTACT *see* Early European Contact; European Contact; Macassan and pre-European Contact; Race Relations

D
DALY RIVER
Stanner
DARETON
Bruell; Busby *et al.*
DARLING BASIN
Allen, H. R. (1972)
DAVENPORT
De Lawyer
DEATH *see* Life Cycle — Sickness, etc.
DEMOGRAPHY
Allen, H. R. (1968) ; Barwick; Beckett (1958) ; Bridges; Fink (1960) ; Goddard; Hamilton; Harvey, A.; Keats; Knox; Lawrence; La Jeunesse; Le Sueur; Littlewood; Rose; Smith, L. R.; Stanner (1932) ; Tatz; Thompson, E. W.; Tonkinson, R. (1966) ; White, N. G.
DENTITION *see* Human Biology — Anthropometry, etc.
DEPOPULATION *see* Population Decline
DESCENT *see* Social Organization and Behaviour — Kinship, etc.
DETRIBALIZATION
Beckett (1958) ; Fitzgerald; Ostapchuk
DIERI LANGUAGE
Trefrey
DINGO
Macintosh
DIVISION OF LABOUR *see* Women's Life — Secular Aspects
DJAMINDJUNG LANGUAGE
Cleverly
DJINGILI LANGUAGE
Chadwick
DREAMS *see* Human Biology — Psychology, etc.

DRYSDALE RIVER MISSION
Eggleston, H. J.
DYIRBAL LANGUAGE
Dixon

E

EARLY EUROPEAN CONTACT
Allen, F. J.; Allen, H. R. (1972); Ashton; Birtles; Biskup; Bladel; Bridges; Brown, H.; Bury; Buxton; Campbell, I. C.; Carlyon; Clarke; Corris; Cowin; Crawford (1969); Curthoys; Dignan; Dunton; Fenn Lusher; Fink (1960); Fitzgerald; Galloway; Gannan; Gibbs; Gibson; Goleby; Graves; Greenway; Harrison, B. W.; Hartwig (1965); Hassell; Hormann; Hunt; Krastins; Loos (1971, 1976); Marcard; Murray-Prior; Nelson; Nolan; Patterson; Pearson; Prentis; Quinlivan; Russo; Smith, B. W.; Sokoloff; Stanner; Taylor, J. C.

ECONOMIC DEVELOPMENT
Beckett (1963); Eckermann; Gibson; Hanson; Hinton; Monk; Robinson (1973); Rogers, P. H.; Snooks; Stanner (1938); Turner; West, A. L.; Wilson, J. (1961); Wilson, K.

ECONOMIC LIFE *see* Material Culture and Ecology

EDUCATION
Barker, R. J.; Barwick; Beckenham; Brock; Burrage; Campbell, R.; Davies; Deakin; Duncan; Edwards, N. R.; Elias; Flood, J. B.; Giles; Goddard; Grant; Harries; Harrison, M.; Hart, A. M.; Hassell; Hunt; Huntsman; Jepsen; Kewal; Lindstrom; McDonnell; McKeich (1971); Mortlock; Nailon; Nettle; Nicholson; Palmer; Patching; Peacock; Prideaux (1971); Quine; Randell; Readdy; Rennie; Reynolds, Peter (1973); Scott; Sherwood; Small; Sommerlad (1972); Trudinger; Tully; Waddington; Walster; Waters; West, A. L.; West, A. H.; Young

EDUCATION — ABORIGINAL STUDIES
Harrison, M.; Nettle

EDUCATION — ACHIEVEMENT
Peak; Quine

EDUCATION — ADULT
Breen, R. M. (1976)

EDUCATION — BILINGUAL
Birdsall; Edmunds; Hart, A. M.; McEvedy; Pohlner; Sherwood

EDUCATION — COMMUNITY
Flood, J. B.

EDUCATION — CURRICULUM
Chambers; Harrison, M.; Nettle

EDUCATION — ETHNIC
Goodale; Hamilton; Hart, A. M.; Jolles; Kok; Quisenberry; Salter

EDUCATION — LEARNING DIFFICULTIES
Waddington

EDUCATION — MOTIVATION AND ATTITUDES
Cummings; Davidson, J. A.; Huntsman; Kennedy; McKeich (1971);
Peacock; Peak; Prideaux (1971); Sommerlad (1972); Watts

EDUCATION — PRE-SCHOOL
Birdsall; Cummings; Harries; Knapman

EDUCATION — TECHNICAL AND VOCATIONAL
Dix; Grant; Rogers, P. H.; Small; Tatz; West, A. L.

EDUCATION — TRADITIONAL
Palmer; Todd

EDUCATIONAL PSYCHOLOGY *see* Psychological Testing

EDWARD RIVER TRIBE
Hall, A. H. (1972)

EMPLOYMENT
Beckett (1958); Bolton; Brown, H.; Buxton; Dalton (1959); Dignan; Fink
(1955); Hilliker; Hinton; Kitson; Le Sueur; McDonnell; McMath;
McPheat; Rogers, C.; Rogers, P. H.; Roy; Snooks; Stanton; Sturkey; Tatz;
Tonkinson, R. (1962); West, A. L.; Wilson, J.; Wilson, K.

ENVIRONMENT, ADAPTATION TO, *see* Material Culture and Ecology

ETHNOHISTORY
Allen, H. R.; Belshaw; Bickford; Brayshaw; Coutts; Crawford (1958); Ellis,
R. W.; Fraser; Hill; Kabo; Lane; Loos (1971); Lourandos; McBryde;
Meagher (1976); Moore; Pearson; Pierce; Poiner; Sabine; Sokoloff;
Sullivan; Wundersitz

EUROPEAN CONTACT *see also* Race Relations
Armstrong, R. E. M.; Bain; Baker; Beckett (1958); Biskup; Calley (1955,
1959); Cawte; Collings; Deakin; Dryburgh; Evans, K. E.; Evans, R. L.;
Fink; Fitzgerald; Gale; Hart, P. R.; Hartwig; Krastins; Milich; Stanner

EVOLUTION
Chase; Cross; Oldmeadow

EXCAVATIONS *see* Archaeology — Camp Sites, etc.

F

FAMILY
Beckett (1958); Biddle; Henderson; Le Sueur; Littlewood; McLean; Makin;
Malinowski; Masengarb; Rogers, C.; Teasdale, J. I.; Watts

FERTILITY RITES *see* Rituals — General

FLYNN, JOHN
McPheat

FOOD — HUNTING, FOOD GATHERING, INTERFERENCE WITH
NATURAL RESOURCES
Allen, H. R.; Bell, D. R.; Bowdler; Coleman; Crawford; Flood, J. M.

(1973); Hardley; Hellsbusch; Hess; Lane; Moore, David R.; Mountford (1962); Pierce; Poiner; Reim; Sadler; Sokoloff; Sullivan; Ter Weer

FOOD — TYPES, COOKING, PREPARING
Allen, H. R.; Bickford; Blaess; Campbell, T. D.; Coleman; Cran; Moore, David R.; Murphy (1961); Pierce; Poiner; Reim; Sabine; Sokoloff; Sullivan; Thompson, E. W.; Worsley

FRINGE DWELLERS *see* Urbanization

G

GAMES AND PASTIMES
Bakker; De Lemos; Hillman; Hye-Kerkdal; Leatch; Prideaux (1971); Salter

GERARD ABORIGINAL RESERVE
Fitzgerald

GIDJINGALI TRIBE
Meehan (1976)

GIN GIN DISTRICT
Dignan

GIPPS, GEORGE
Patterson; Reece

GIYUM LANGUAGE
South

GNOWANGERUP TRIBE
Slarke

GOGO-YIMIDJIR LANGUAGE
De Zwaan (1967, 1969)

GOVERNMENT POLICY, NINETEENTH CENTURY
Biskup; Bladel; Bridges; Clarke; Cowin; Duncan; Dunton, J. M.; Galloway; Hart, A. M.; Hasluck; Hassell; Hetherington; Hickey; Hoskins; Hunt; Johnston; Marcard; Marchant; Patterson; Reece; Shelmerdine; Walsh; Welborn; Willmington

GOVERNMENT POLICY, TWENTIETH CENTURY
Bakker; Barwick; Beatty; Biskup; Brock; Brodie; Burnard; De Lawyer; Duncan; Edwards, D.; Edwards, N. R.; Farmer, R. L.; Fink (1955); Gibson; Hart, A. M.; Harvey, A.; Hetherington; Hickey; Johansons; Le Sueur; Lockley; Lovejoy; Milich; Patching; Paterson; Small; Tatz; Warhurst; Whitworth

GROOTE EYLANDT
Lawn; Moody (1954); Rose; Turner

GUGADA LANGUAGE
Platt

GUGU-BADHUN LANGUAGE
Sutton

GUJANI LANGUAGE
Hercus

HUMAN BIOLOGY — NUTRITIONAL STUDIES, HEALTH AND DISEASE
Campbell, T. D.; Coolican; Cran; Good; Hackett; Hargrave; Kamien; Kidson; Kirke; Lickiss; McCooke; Moodie

HUMAN BIOLOGY — PHYSICAL CHARACTERISTICS, RACIAL COMPARISONS
Adam, W.; Bain; Brisbout; Brown, T. (1967); Campbell, T. D.; Craven; Davidson, G. R.; De Lemos; De Zwaan; Gallimore; Kearney; Keats; Kennedy; Kidson; Killington; Kuusk; Lai; Lendon; Lindstrom; Macintosh; Murphy (1957); Petersen; Randell; Rao; Thorne; Tulsi; Watts; White, N. G.

HUMAN BIOLOGY — PSYCHOLOGY (INCLUDING DREAMS)
Cawte; Christophers; Davidson, G. R.; De Lemos; Denham; Hausfeld (1972); Kennedy; Kommers; Leatch; Malot; Pentony; Thompson, E. W.; Williams, D.; Wolkenberg

HUNTING *see* Food — Hunting, etc.

I

IDENTITY, PERSONAL AND GROUP
Bicknell; Cake; Fitzpatrick; Forby (1970); Jepsen; Killington; Kok; McKeich (1971); Makin; Mundy; Myers; Peak; Pierson; Robinson (1973); Roy; Sommerlad; Taragel

INFANTICIDE *see* Life Cycle — General, etc.

IMPLEMENTS AND QUARRIES
Adam, L.; Allen, F. J.; Allen, H. R.; Anell; Ashbolt; Bauer; Bickford; Blaess; Boness; Brisbout; Bowdler; Cooper; Coutts; Flood, J. M.; Glover; Hess; Hill; Hume; Kamminga; Kelly; McBryde; Macintosh; Mistrate-Haarhuis; Morphy; Pearce (1972); Pope; Struwe (1974); Sullivan, B. M.; Townley; White, C.; Yalden

INDULKANA
Reid, S. C.

INDUSTRIAL RELATIONS
Stevens

INSTITUTIONS (HOMES, HOSTELS, PRISONS)
Cake; Christophers; Kewal; McKeich (1961); Robinson (1967); Sommerlad (1972); Tilbrook; Trainor

INTELLIGENCE TESTS *see* Human Biology — Physical Characteristics, etc.

INTEGRATION
Brock; Brodie; Marchant; Rogers, C.; Roy; Sommerlad (1968)

INTER-GROUP RELATIONS (INCLUDING TRADE AND EXCHANGE)
see also Hostilities
Bell, J. H.; Belshaw; Bickford; Brown, T. A.; Fine; Fink (1960); Fletcher; Flood, J. M. (1973); Loverock; McCarthy; Micha; Moore, David R.; Powell, T. M.; Ter Weer; Tonkinson, R. (1972); Turner; Worsley

LAKE MUNGO
Barbetti; Thorne (1975)

LAND RIGHTS *see* Politics, Aboriginal (including land rights)

LANGUAGE AND COMMUNICATION — ABORIGINAL ENGLISH
Alexander; Dutton; Readdy

LANGUAGE AND COMMUNICATION — GENERAL (INCLUDING SIGN
LANGUAGE, MESSAGE STICKS)
Blaess; De Zwaan; Fischer-Colbrie; Frank; Gillen; Hamilton; Mitchell, I. S.;
Moody (1953); Morphy; O'Grady (1959); See; South

LANGUAGE AND COMMUNICATION — GRAMMAR, PHONOLOGY,
VOCABULARIES
Alpher; Birk; Blake; Brasch; Breen, J. G.; Brisbout; Calley (1959);
Chadwick; Cleverly; Cunningham; De Zwaan; Dixon; Hall, A. H.; Harris,
J. J. K.; Keen; Kilham; Love; Metcalfe (1972); Moody (1954); Oates;
Osborne; Platt; Quisenberry; Schebeck; See; Sommer; Strehlow; Sutton;
Trefrey; Tsunoda; Worsley; Yallop

LANGUAGE AND COMMUNICATION — PSYCHOLINGUISTIC
DEVELOPMENT
Barker, R. J.; Elias; Foggitt; Harries; Teasdale, G. R.

LANGUAGE AND COMMUNICATION — TEXT AND TRANSLATIONS
Breen, J. G.; Chadwick; De Zwaan (1969); Dixon; Ellis, C. J.; Fink (1960);
Hall, A. H.; Keen; Love; Oates; Quisenberry; Sutton; Yallop

LA PEROUSE
Beauchamp; Bell, J. H.; Nixon

LAW — ABORIGINAL INVOLVEMENT WITH
Beckett (1958); Bern; Bridges; Corris; Dunton; Eggleston, E. M.; Hassell;
Johnston; Lemaire; Makin; Robinson (1967); Taylor, J. C.; Williams, N.M.

LAWS PERTAINING TO ABORIGINES
Beckett (1958); Bridges; Burnard; Eggleston, E. M.; Graves; Harvey, A.;
Johnston; Philp; Sheehan; Williams, N.M.

LEPROSY
Goss; Hargrave

LIFE CYCLE — GENERAL (INCLUDING CONCEPTION BELIEFS,
BIRTH, INFANTICIDE, CHILDHOOD)
Calley (1959); Denham; Fratkin; Goodale; Hamilton; Jolles; Kewal; Kirke;
Lickiss; McLean; Meagher (1976); Montagu; Mountford (1962); Richter;
Ryan, D'A. J.; Ter Weer; Thompson, E. W.; Tonkinson, R. (1966);
Williams, D.

LIFE CYCLE — MARRIAGE AND SEXUAL RELATIONS
Beckett (1958); Calley (1955, 1959); Farnhill; Goodale; Grau; Hiatt, L. R.
(1962); Littlewood; Rammer; Rose; Sackett; Shapiro; Stanner (1932);
West, A. L.; Wunderly; Wyllie

LIFE CYCLE — SICKNESS, INJURY (INCLUDING TREATMENT), OLD
AGE, DEATH
Cawte; Coolican; Drobec; Fenner; Goodale; Guariglia; Hackett; Kirke;
Sieber; Tonkinson, R. (1966); Wunderly

LITERATURE, ABORIGINES IN
Cowell; Gray, J. C.; Healy; Jones, D. L. M.; Kershaw; Melandres;
Richardson; Saxby; Van Gent (1969)

LOWER BURNETT DISTRICT
Dignan

M

MACASSAN AND PRE-EUROPEAN CONTACT
Crawford (1969); Hiatt, L. R. (1962); Krastins; Macknight; Moore, David
R.; Sellick; Worsley

MACINTYRE VALLEY
Pearson

McLEAY VALLEY
Campbell, V. R.

MADI MADI LANGUAGE
Hercus

MAGIC *see* Religion and Magic

MALAK MALAK LANGUAGE
Birk

MANGAT
Sullivan, K. M. (1973)

MANINGRIDA
Armstrong, G.; Hart, J. A.; Hiatt, L. R. (1962)

MARI LANGUAGE
Beale

MARANOA
Brown, H.

MARRIAGE *see* Social Organisation and Behaviour   Kinship; etc.

MATERIAL CULTURE AND ECOLOGY
Allen, H. R.; Bakhta; Bartholomeusz; Belshaw; Bickford; Bowdler;
Brayshaw; Campbell, T. D. (1939); Corris; Crawford; Dryburgh; Ellis,
R. W.; Fink (1960); Fletcher; Flood, J. M. (1973); Gannan; Grandowski;
Hardley; Hellsbusch; Hiatt, B.; Hughes; Lane; Lawrence; Lourandos;
McBryde; McCarthy; Montagu; Moore, David R.; Mountford (1962);
Ostapchuk; Pearson; Pierce; Poiner; Reynolds, Peter (1973); Sabine;
Sharp; Sokoloff; Stanner; Sullivan, B. M. (1964); Turner; Worsley

MEDICINE MEN *see* Religion and Magic

MELBOURNE, ABORIGINES IN
Barwick; Edwards, D.; Randolph; Taragel

MELVILLE ISLAND *see* Tiwi

MENTAL CHARACTERISTICS *see* Human Biology — Physical Characteristics, etc.

MESSAGE STICKS *see* Language and Communications — General, etc.

MIDDENS *see* Archaeology — Camp Sites, etc.

MIGRATION INTO AND WITHIN AUSTRALIA
Bartholomeusz; Bauer; Bicknell; Davidson, D. S. (1928); Guthrie; Macintosh; Tang; White, N. G.

MIRNING
Marun

MISSIONS
Adams, E. J.; Ashton; Blaess; Bridges; Bull; Burnard; Bury; Calley (1955); Cook; Corris; Cowin; Crawford (1969); Deakin; De Lacey; De Lawyer; De Zwaan (1969); Edwards, N. R.; Evans, K. E.; Gibson; Hart, A. M.; Hart, P. R.; Hartwig (1965); Hickey; Hinton; Lawn; McPheat; Marks; Minchen; Moody (1953); Nelson; Northey; O'Kelly; Rankin; Rayner; Reece; Robin; Robinson (1973); Russo; Sampson; Schmeichen; Stanner (1932); Tatz; Tonkinson, R.; Van Geffen; Walsh; West, A. L.; Wyllie

MITCHELL RIVER
Crim

MOGUMBER METHODIST TRAINING CENTRE
Cook

MOORA
Roy

MOORE RIVER
Scott

MUNGGAN LANGUAGE
Kilham

MURCHISON DISTRICT
Fink (1960)

MURNGIN TRIBE
Blows; Lathbury; Layton; Peterson; Plummer; Shapiro; White, N. G.

MURRAY RIVER
Wundersitz

MURRAY VALLEY
Bickford

MURWILLUMBAH
Martyn

MUSIC AND SONGS
Ellis, C. J.; Fink (1960); Hagen, K.; Jones, T. A.; Lowrey; McCardell; Moyle; Quisenberry; Reid, S. C.; Rosier; Shannon; Wild; Marit

MYALL CREEK MASSACRE
Campbell, I. C.; Collings; Flood, J. B.; Harrison, B. W.; Reece

MYTHOLOGY *see also* Rainbow Serpent
Blows; Brandl, E. J.; Calley (1952); D'Espeissis; Glass; Lathbury; Layton; Maddock; Meagher (1960); Morphy; Mountford (1962); Quisenberry; Tully; Visser; Wilpert

N

NAMBUCCA
Lane

NARROGIN
Carr; Metcalfe (1960); Tonkinson, R. (1962)

NATIVE POLICE
Cowin; Nelson; Reece; Shelmerdine; Taylor, N.

NATURAL RESOURCES, INTERFERENCE WITH, *see* Food — Hunting, etc.

NEW ENGLAND DISTRICT, ABORIGINES IN
Belshaw; Campbell, I. C.; Flood, J. B.; McBryde; Murray-Prior

NEW NORCIA
Russo; Watson

NEW SOUTH WALES, ABORIGINES IN
Beckett (1958); Belshaw; Bridges; Burrage; Calley (1955); Campbell, R.; Cummings; Curthoys; Duncan; Dunton; Goleby; Harries; Iredale; Jennett (1966); Johnston; Kilkelly; Knox; Le Sueur; Peak; Pöch; Poiner; Prentis; Reay; Reece; Sullivan, S. M. (1970); Swan; Vallance

NGARRINDJERI TRIBE
Jenkins

NGIYARI/LANGKA CYCLE
Reid, S. C.

NORTHERN TERRITORY, ABORIGINES IN
Blows; Edmunds; Edwards; Hart, A. M.; Hilliker; Holm; Johansons; Moody (1953); O'Kelly; Pilling; Stanner; Tatz; Williams; Wyllie

NULLABOR PLAIN
Marun

NUTRITIONAL STUDIES *see* Human Biology — Nutritional Studies, etc.

NYANUMATA LANGUAGE
O'Grady (1963)

NYOONGAH TRIBE
Howard

O

OLD AGE *see* Life Cycle - - Sickness, etc.

ORGANIZATIONS, ABORIGINAL OR CONCERNED WITH ABORIGINES
Jennett (1970); Middleton; Pierson; Surman; Taragel; Wilson, J. (1961)

OSTEOLOGY
Thorne (1975)

P

PALLOTINE TRAINING CENTRE
Mulholland

PALM ISLAND
Dutton

PARNKALA TRIBE
Fischer-Colbrie

PEARLING INDUSTRY
Shepherd; Wilmott

PERTH, ABORIGINES IN
Dunne; Henderson; McCooke; McKeich (1961); Makin; Metcalfe (1960); Mortlock; Mutton; Powell, G. M.; Randolph; Thompson, E. W.; Tilbrook

PHONOLOGY *see* Language and Communications — Grammar, etc.

PHYSICAL CHARACTERSITICS *see* Human Biology — Physical Characteristics, etc.

PILBARA
McCardell

PINDAN
Wilson, J. (1961); Wilson, K.

PINJARRA
Bell, K. J.; Storer

PITJANDJARA *see* Bidjanjadjara

PLAY — CHILDREN'S, *see* Games and Pastimes

POINT McLEAY ABORIGINAL MISSION
Bury

POINT PEARCE
Ostapchuk; Peacock

POLITICS, ABORIGINAL (INCLUDING LAND RIGHTS)
Beckett (1963); Bern; Brodie; Hocking; Hoffman, T. D.; Howard; Jennett (1970); Lester; Middleton; Surmon; Wilson, J.

POPULATION DECLINE
Bridges; Campbell, I. C.; Hormann; Johnston; Prentis; Wyllie

PORTRAITS, ABORIGINAL
Buscombe

PORT AUGUSTA
Klem

PORT ESSINGTON
Allen, F. J.

PORT KEATS
Falkenberg

PORT PHILLIP DISTRICT
Nelson; Shelmerdine

PORT PHILLIP PROTECTORATE
Ashton; Harris, D.

PORT STEPHENS
Sokoloff

POVERTY AND MATERIAL DEPRIVATION
Beckenham; Biddle; Chia; Cummings; Dalton; Forby; Goddard; Hanson; Kirke; Le Sueur; Loverock; Makin; Mazengarb; Mutton; Powell, G. M.; Roy

PREHISTORY
Kabo; Long; Piper; Thorne (1975)

PROTECTORS AND PROTECTORATES, ABORIGINAL
Ashton; Campbell, I. C.; Carlyon; Galloway; Johnston; Nelson; Reece

PSYCHIATRIC ILLNESS *see* Human Biology — Psychology

PSYCHOLOGICAL TESTING
Barker, R. J.; Dasen; Davidson, G. R. (1971); Davidson, J. A.; De Lacey; De Lemos; Farmer, R. G.; Fink (1955); Fisher; Foggitt; Gallimore; Harries; Harrigan; Hart, J. A.; Hausfeld (1972); Hillman; Holm; Huntsman; Karathanasis; Kearney; Kennedy; Lindstrom; McKeich (1971); Nicholson; Peacock; Peak; Petersen; Prideaux; Randell; Smith, K. K.; Stewart; Teasdale, G. R.; Watts

PSYCHOLOGY *see* Human Biology — Psychology

PUKAMANI CEREMONY
Brandl, M. M.; Goodale

PUNISHMENT, CAPITAL — QUEENSLAND
Barber

Q

QUARRIES *see* Implements and Quarries

QUEENSLAND, ABORIGINES IN
Barber; Cowlin; Halliwell; Hardley; Evans, R. L.; Hoskins; Lauer; Lockley; McDonnell; Rayner; Sharp; Taylor, J. C.; Thomson (1951)

R

RACE RELATIONS
Bain; Beatty; Beauchamp; Campbell, I. C.; Chambers; Cowell; Cowin; Dalton (1964); Denholm; Edwards, D.; Evans, K. E.; Evans, R. L.; Fink (1955); Flood, J. B.; Galloway; Gibbs; Graves; Harrison, B. W.; Harrison, C. M. A.; Hartwig; Harvey, A.; Harvey, S. W.; Hasluck; Hassell; Hausfeld (1960); Henwood; Hillman; Hogan; Howell; Jennett; Kilkelly; Loos;

Loverock; Maranta; Markus; McPheat; Mundy; Prentis; Prideaux; Rayner; Reece; Reid, B. J.; Rennie; Robbins; Rosewarne; Shaw; Slarke; Snooks; Stanton; Stevens; Storer; Surmon; Taal; Taylor, J. C.; Tilby; West, A. L.; Wilson, J. (1958)

RACE RELATIONS — DISCRIMINATION AND PREJUDICE
Bell; Bennett; Cake; Collings; Curthoys; Ellis, M. R.; Gale; Graves; Hagen, R.; Hall, J. R.; Hassell; Jennett; Klem; Le Sueur; Markus; Middleton; Murray-Prior; Philp; Reece; Reid, B. J.; Rogers, P. H.; Roy; Stone; Vallance; Wolkenberg.

RACIAL COMPARISONS, HUMAN BIOLOGY *see* Human Biology — Physical Characteristics, etc.

RADIO CARBON DATING
Barbetti

RAINBOW SERPENT *see also* Mythology
Breen, R. M. (1969); Calley; Deering; Triebels

RELIGION — BELIEFS AND VALUES
Bain; Blaess; Boyall; Breen, R. M. (1969); Calley; Corris; Crawford (1969); Haude; Hellsbusch; Kotz; Myers; Nailon; Ralph; Ryan, D'A. J.; Sharp; Wanninger; Wilpert; Worsley

RELIGION AND MAGIC (INCLUDING MEDICINE MEN)
Calley; Deering; Drobec; Gillen; Guariglia; Hellsbusch; Kommers; Lanquist; Rosier; Ryan, D'A. J.; Thompson, D. F.; Tonkinson, R. (1966); Van Gent (1967); Villiers; Worsley

REMBARNGA LANGUAGE
McKay

RICHMOND RIVER
Sullivan, S. M. (1964)

RITUALS — GENERAL
Adam, L.; Allen, H. R. (1972); Blaess; Blows; Brandl, M. M.; Breen, R. M. (1969); Calley; Fine; Fink (1960); Fraser; Gillen; Kaberry; Lathbury; Maddock; Moore, David R.; Ryan, D'A. J.; Sullivan; Tonkinson, R.; Von Timm

RITUALS — INITIATION *see also* Rituals — General
Blows; Brandl, E. J.; Davidson, D. S. (1928); Fratkin; Goodale; Hiatt, L. R. (1962); Kommers; O'Grady (1959); Thompson, D. F.; Twyman; Worsley

RITUALS — MORTUARY RITES AND PRACTICES *see also* Rituals — General
Akerman; Blaess; Boorsboom; Brandl, M. M.; Goodale; Haglund-Calley; Hiatt, L. R. (1962); King-Boyes; Meehan, B. F.; Worsley

RITUALS — WOMEN'S RITUALS
Calley (1959); Goodale; Kaberry; McLean; Maddock; Quisenberry; Reynolds, Patricia; Rosier; Shannon

RIVERINA DISTRICT
Buxton

ROBINSON, G. H.
Carlyon
ROCKHAMPTON
Halliwell
ROCKY CAPE
Jones, R.
ROSSMOYNE
Mullholland

S

SALMON GUMS
Young
SALVADO, BISHOP
Russo
SCHOOLS — COMMUNITY RELATIONS
Bamborough; Flood, J. B.; Williams
SETTLEMENTS AND RESERVES
Alexander (1965); Armstrong; Bakker; Barwick; Beckett (1958); Bridges;
De Lawyer; Fink (1955); Fitzgerald; Hanson; Hausfeld (1960); Hoskins;
Johansons; Johnston; Ostapchuk; Oxer; Pierson; Savarton and George;
Wilson, J. (1958)
SIGN LANGUAGE *see* Language and Communication — General, etc.
SOCIAL DEVIANCE
Lickiss; Robinson; Stockbridge; Trainor
SOCIAL ORGANIZATION AND BEHAVIOUR — GENERAL
Allen, H. R. (1972); Armstrong; Bakhta; Beckett (1963); Blaess; Brandl,
E. J.; Calley (1959); Corris; Crawford (1969); Davidson, D. S. (1924);
Denham; Dyke; Eckermann; Fink (1960); Fletcher; Gibson; Grandowski;
Gray, G. R.; Haraesser; Hausfeld (1960); Hiatt, L. R. (1962); Howell;
Kaberry; Kommers; Layton; Leatch; Love; Loverock; Massey; Meggitt;
Monk; Moody (1953); Moore, David R.; Muldoon; Peterson; Quisenberry;
Reynolds, Peter (1973); Sabine; Sharp; Sokoloff; Stanner (1932);
Tonkinson, R. (1966); Turner; Wilson, J.; Worsley
SOCIAL ORGANIZATION AND BEHAVIOUR — KINSHIP, DESCENT,
MARRIAGE GROUPING, CLANS etc.
Adams; Armstrong; Barwick; Brandl, M. M.; Calley (1959); Crim; Ellis,
C. J.; Falkenberg; Farnhill; Gray, G. R.; Hiatt, L. R. (1962); Jackes;
Lucich; Mazengarb; Meggitt; Noon; Plummer; Rose; Ryan, D'A. J.;
Sackett; Shapiro; Sharp; Terwiel-Powel; Testart; Thomson; Tonkinson, R.
(1966); Von Guhr; Von Sturmer
SOCIAL WELFARE *see* Community Welfare
SOCIAL WORK *see* Community Welfare
SOCIETY OF FRIENDS — QUEENSLAND
Lauer

SOCIO-CULTURAL DEPRIVATION
Bakker; Beckenham; Biddle; Chia; Cummings; De Lacey; De Lemos; Duncan; Forby; Giles; Goddard; Jepsen; Kennedy; Kewal; Leatch; Loverock; McKeich (1971); Makin; Peak; Philp; Teasdale, G. R.

SOUTH AUSTRALIA, ABORIGINES IN
Brock; Brodie; Burnard; Gale; Gibbs; Hart, A. M.; Hassell; Milich; Rammer; Walsh

SUNDAY ISLAND
Gibson

SWAN HILL
Gannan

SWAN RIVER
Green

SYDNEY, ABORIGINES IN
Beauchamp; Bell, J. H.; Iredale; Larsen; Lickiss; Nixon; Randolph; Sommerlad (1968); Surmon

SYMBOLISM *see* Rituals; Mythology; Totemism

T

TASMANIAN ABORIGINES
Adam, W.; Bladel; Cross; Featherstone; Hiatt, B.; Hormann; Hughes; Jones, R.; Lourandos; Macintosh; Meumann; Nicholls; Ryan, L.; Thorne (1967); Völger; Wunderly

THAAYOOR LANGUAGE
Hall, A. H.

THURSDAY ISLAND
Evans, G.

TINGHA
Baker

TIWI TRIBE
Brandl, M. M.; Goodale; Hackett; Krastins; Osborne; Pilling; White, N. G.

TIWI LANGUAGE
Osborne

TJURUNGA
Meagher (1960); Tonkinson, J. R.; Wanninger

TOOLS — STONE
Pearce, R. H.

TORRES STRAIT ISLANDS
Beckett (1963); Evans, G.; Fraser

TORRES STRAIT ISLANDS — EDUCATION
Finch

TOTEMISM
Bain; Barker, G. H.; Brown, M. W.; Crisp; De Graaf; Dyke; Ellis;

Knowles; Morley; Reynolds, Peter (1962); Ryan, D'A. J.; Sharp; Smythe; Thompson, D. F.; Tully; Vatter

TRADE AND EXCHANGE see Inter-Group Relations, etc.

TREPANG INDUSTRY
Macknight

TRIBAL LAW
Boyall; Eggleston, E. M.; Pilling; Taylor, J. C.; Tonkinson (1966)

TWEED VALLEY
Piper; Sullivan, S. M. (1964)

TYNTYNDER
Gannan

U

UMEEWARRA
De Lawyer

UMI:DA TRIBE
Blundell

URBANIZATION see also Assimilation
Baker; Beauchamp; Beckett; Bell, J. H.; Bicknell; Biddle; Breen, R. M. (1976); Clark; Dalton (1964); Edwards, D.; Fink (1955); Forby; Gale; Hall, J. R.; Harvey, A.; Henderson; Henwood; Iredale; Killington; Klem; Larsen; Lickiss; McKeich; Makin; Metcalfe (1960); Mitchell, B. J.; Mutton; Nixon; Pierson; Powell, G. M.; Randolph; Rogers, C.; Roy; Shaw; Slarke; Taragel; Thompson, P. J.; Tomlinson; Trainor; Vallance; Wait; Wolkenberg

V

VALUE ORIENTATION
Eckermann

VICTORIA, ABORIGINES IN
Corris; Galloway; Marcard

VISUAL ARTS AND CRAFTS
Adam, L.; Allen, H. R. (1972); Brandl, E. J.; Brice; Calley (1952); Dallas; D'Espeissis, Frank, Fraser; Griffith; Hart, E. J.; King-Boyes; Kupka; Macintosh; McMah; Meagher; Mistrate-Haarhuis; Moore, David R.; Morphy; Mountford; Munn; Pope; Sellick; Sharpe; Tonkinson, J. R.; Von Timm; Weigl; West, M. K. C.

VOCABULARIES see Language and Communications — Grammar, etc.

W

WAGES POLICY
Hilliker

WALGETT
Bamborough; Jepson

WALJBIRI TRIBE
Brown, T.; Fine; Grave; Hiatt, L. R. (1957); Kuusk; Meggitt; Munn; Rao (1970); Schulze; Shannon

WALUWARA LANGUAGE
Breen, J. G.

WANINDILJAUGWA TRIBE
Worsley

WANUNGAMAGALJUAGBA
Turner

WARBURTON RANGES
Sluggett

WARUNGU LANGUAGE
Tsunoda

WATTIE CREEK
Middleton

WAUWILOK MYTH
Blows; Breen, R. M. (1969); Calley (1952); Glass; Lathbury

WEAPONS *see also* Implements
Fischer-Colbrie; Hess; Howe; Kelly; Lenoch; Moore, David R.

WEILMORINGLE
Savarton and George

WELLUMBIN
Martyn

WESTERN AUSTRALIA, ABORIGINES IN
Biskup; Goodard; Hall, J. R.; Hasluck; Henderson; Hickey; Kitson; McKeich; Marchant; Marks; O'Grady (1959); Patching; Paterson; Randell; Rankin; Robertson; Sampson; Shaw; Small; Stockbridge; Welborn; West, A. H.

WIKMUNKAN TRIBE
Adams; Jackes; Kilham; Thomson (1951)

WILCANNIA
Savarton and George

WILSON'S PROMONTORY
Coutts; Hope, G. S.

WILUNA
Sackett

WOMEN'S LIFE (RITUAL) *see* Rituals — Women's Rituals

WOMEN'S LIFE — SECULAR ASPECTS (INCLUDING DIVISION OF LABOUR, STATUS) •
Belshaw; Bickford; Blaess; Bowdler; Cawte; Goodale; Harrigan; Kaberry; McLean; Moore, David R.; Shapiro; Sokoloff; Teasdale, J. I.; Wilson, K.; Wyllie